The Last Kingdom Standing

The Last Kingdom Standing

Hope for a World in Crisis

ROBERT SCHMIDT
foreword by Roger Finke

WIPF & STOCK · Eugene, Oregon

THE LAST KINGDOM STANDING
Hope for a World in Crisis

Copyright © 2024 Robert Schmidt. All rights reserved. Except for brief quotations in critical publications or reviews, no part of this book may be reproduced in any manner without prior written permission from the publisher. Write: Permissions, Wipf and Stock Publishers, 199 W. 8th Ave., Suite 3, Eugene, OR 97401.

Wipf & Stock
An Imprint of Wipf and Stock Publishers
199 W. 8th Ave., Suite 3
Eugene, OR 97401

www.wipfandstock.com

PAPERBACK ISBN: 979-8-3852-1578-2
HARDCOVER ISBN: 979-8-3852-1579-9
EBOOK ISBN: 979-8-3852-1580-5

VERSION NUMBER 08/28/24

Scripture quotations are from New Revised Standard Version (NRSV), copyright © 1989 National Council of the Churches of Christ in the United States of America. Used by permission. All rights reserved worldwide.

To the beloved memory of Karin,
courageous companion in international service

Contents

Foreword by Roger Finke | *ix*

Preface | *xi*

Acknowledgments | *xiii*

Introduction | 1

Chapter 1	When God Was King	13
Chapter 2	Politics on Trial	22
Chapter 3	Lamentation and Promises	31
Chapter 4	The Kingdom of God Is Near	43
Chapter 5	The Kingdom in Cross and Conflict	55
Chapter 6	The Kingdom in Crises	65
Chapter 7	Good News in Trying Times	73
Chapter 8	God's New World Society	82
Chapter 9	Coercion vs. Consensus	94
Chapter 10	Amazement and Energizing	106
Chapter 11	The Church in Exile	117
Chapter 12	The Evangelism of Jesus	127

Conclusion | 137

Bibliography | *143*

Foreword

THIS BOOK REPRESENTS A LIFELONG journey of exploration for Dr. Robert Schmidt. As a pastor and theologian, with a doctorate in political science, he has sought to explain how biblical teachings and principles should remain a source of hope and inspiration for the most challenging problems of today. In homilies, classrooms, and research publications, he has tried out his ideas with parishioners, students, and political science scholars. This book is the culmination of his journey.

So, what is his source of hope? Building on the work of many theologians, he explains how the "Kingdom of God," so frequently referenced in the Gospels, is that source of hope. He carefully explains that this Kingdom is not defined as the *reign of God* but rather as the *providence of God* and explains how this God works throughout history. For Schmidt, his emphasis on the Kingdom of God is not a call for a new mission, but rather a return to the mission outlined in the Gospels and throughout the Bible.

The entire book is a challenge to clergy, churches, and the Christian community to live out this mission. Throughout the book Dr. Schmidt carefully lays out the biblical foundation for the Kingdom of God mission and then applies this mission to the challenges of today. As in his ministry as a pastor and his research as a political scientist, his focus is global and is carefully couched within history.

Like many proposals built on core biblical teachings, the mission he offers is brave, bold, and often troubling. Some will disagree with his political assessments, historical reviews, and theological interpretations, but Christians should not ignore his challenge or shy away from joining him on this journey. For anyone valuing the teachings of the Christian Bible, understanding and applying the Kingdom of God on earth is a challenge that must be met. Dr. Schmidt writes: "[a] contemporary look at the Kingdom

Foreword

may signal hope for the world and a new direction for the Church." For all Christians, the Kingdom of God should always be a source of hope.

ROGER FINKE
Distinguished Professor Emeritus of Sociology, Religious Studies and International Affairs, Pennsylvania State University

Preface

IN OUR FIRST WEEK IN NIGERIA, we were taken to a room in a rural hospital with about thirty children sick and dying from *Kwashiorkor* or protein deficiency. My wife, Karin, was a German refugee who had grown up during the war. I had just graduated from a seminary in St. Louis and was to begin teaching in a seminary in Southern Nigeria. One of my assignments was to teach Christian doctrine and New Testament Greek. How does one relate the seminary curriculum to the children in the hospital, or to the poverty in the villages, unemployment in the towns, or the war experiences of my wife?

Going from being a seminary student to teaching seminary in a new land, they thought I could use some practical experience ministering in a church. So, I was assigned to ten congregations. Teachers from the primary schools would read published sermons and I would be the sacramental pastor baptizing, communing, and confirming new members. Some fellow missionaries served thirty congregations; one had sixty. More African pastors were desperately needed.

To upgrade the educational level of those entering the seminary, potential new students were assisted in completing a high school education. With some extra help, those who were about to enter the seminary received very high marks in their high school examinations and left the seminary program for excellent jobs in the government and business sectors. They had not lost their faith but had lost the connection between ministry in the church and real life.

On a second tour, dealing with a family health issue in Ibadan, I experienced a riot leading up to the Nigerian civil war. In the succeeding month I learned that friends were killed in the carnage. The missionaries came home and the teachers returned to their villages, leaving the congregations on their own. Later we learned that during the war the elders of the churches led their congregations in instruction, prayer, and aid. During the duration of the war, the total membership of the church body more than doubled.

Upon returning the United States I became a campus pastor. Seeking to better understand Africa's civil wars, I studied political science and received doctorate with a dissertation on "The Legitimacy of Revolution: The World Council of Churches Grants to the Liberation Movements of Southern Africa." Later as a professor of theology and political science I sought integrate them to address developing global issues.

Visits to Mexico and Zimbabwe focused on liberation theology in Latin America and Africa. Travel throughout Eastern Europe, Russia, and Ukraine after the fall of communism revealed the tensions of emerging nationalism. Lecturing in Japan, India, and China on social justice and the eucharistic ministry of volunteer clergy gave me new insights on the church life in those nations.

In theology my struggle to relate the Christian message to those children with *Kwashiorkor* and the civil wars in Africa brought me to examine and proclaim Jesus' announcement that the Kingdom of God is at hand. When he told people to believe the "good news," was it protein for kids as well as the hope of heaven? Does peace mean the end of violent conflict as well as the reconciliation between God and us, you and me?

On the political scene it has become evident that nations are no longer in control of what is going on in the world. While they make statements about climate change, the crises are growing. The war in Ukraine, surprising to some at this time in modern history, may simply be the precursor to World War III. Devastating poverty, failed states, and refugees by the millions call for international solutions that at present are lacking.

Is there something the church can do? In the West, young people are leaving, and organized churches are shrinking. If a congregation can no longer pay their pastor, could the elders take over, as they did in Nigeria? Does the church need to spend most of its efforts in keeping the structure going or could it work with what God is doing in realizing God's gifts of the Kingdom? A contemporary look at the Kingdom may signal hope for the world and a new direction for the church.

Acknowledgments

SPECIAL THANKS TO THE STAFF and students at Concordia University in Portland, who helped to refine my thinking on the Kingdom of God for a course called "Faith for the Future." I would also like to thank David Severtson for his help in preparing the proposal for the book, the late Pat Santleman for her literary advice, and my son, Michael, for his counsel and help.

Introduction

PASTOR MIKE LOOKED AT his text again. Jesus said, "The Kingdom of God has come near, repent and believe in the good news" (Mark 1:15). What is the good news? Church attendance never recovered after the pandemic. Last year the denomination lost thousands. When he graduated from the seminary there were 125 graduates. This year there were less than twenty-five. His daughter, Jane, who had been so active in the youth group, had stopped going to church. Now she was more interested in climate change. Most of the members of the church were in their sixties. Unless things changed radically, the congregation would probably close in fifteen or twenty years. Thank God he could retire before then. Back to the text: What is the good news? Is it just heaven?

Pastor Kansa in Ethiopia looked at the same text. There were more people in church now than ever before. Estimates now place the denominational membership at more than eight million. But the land was parched, and many were hungry. There was no work. Now his son, Haro, was struggling to get to Europe. The pastor prayed he would not be lost at sea. When some people came by to beg, what could he give them? There had been no salary for months. His wife cried in the night. What was to become of them? The world was changing; the cattle who died were drying out in the fields. Did no one care? What would he preach about this week? What is the good news? Is it just heaven?

As both pastors delved into the Scriptures, the study of the Kingdom of God began to generate some hope. After Jesus proclaimed the Kingdom, he healed, fed, forgave, challenged the rich, and brought good news to the poor. He praised an enemy officer, commended a despised Samaritan, and raised people from the dead. The Kingdom of God was the fulfillment of the promises of the prophets. Yes, it was about heaven, but also about food, water, healing, forgiveness, home ownership, employment, liberation, and peace between nations. Yes, and to bring about these blessings today, Jesus *is* concerned about climate change, refugees, terrible poverty, and war. Jesus, the Christ, is bringing about these blessings and sometimes he works through us.

WORLD IN TRANSITION

We need his help; problems are growing. There are few happy nations today. Nearly every one of the G7 nations is badly polarized. Inflation, risk of recession, climate crises, threat of war, and porous borders demand political solutions. At the same time governments find themselves powerless to mobilize necessary resources to address the problems. It is even worse in poorer nations. There debt, massive unemployment, poverty, starvation, and armed conflict lead to failed states.

The present world system has few answers to the problems posed by climate change, by hunger, by global underemployment, by endemic poverty, by imprisonment, by lack of medical care, by inadequate housing, and by wars that cause millions of fatalities. For five hundred years we have sought remedies. Individual states like Russia and China and their satellites have tried communism and socialism, but at the world level the problems have increased and are becoming worse. It is time to understand what is happening in our world so that we can live through the coming crises with hope.

The *Foreign Affairs* Centennial Issue called our time "The Age of Uncertainty." An opening article warns of the destructive potential of climate change and nuclear war.[1] Recently Bryant Watson wrote a book titled *Headed into the Abyss*, which warns of imminent collapse and dissolution of our world.[2] Ray Dalio, a hedge fund manager, claims that the times ahead will be radically different from what we know today.[3] Immanuel Wallerstein, a world systems analyst, entitles a book *The End of the World as We Know It*.[4] One reason why people around the world are worried about the future is that the present world system will not be able to meet the rising expectations of the world's people. This in turn will bring about political instability, open conflicts, and civil and interstate wars. Having dominated

---

1. Macaskill, "Beginning of History," 10.
2. Watson, *Headed into the Abyss*, 1.
3. Dalio, *Changing World Order*, 1.
4. Wallerstein, *End of the World*.

Introduction

work and commerce for the past five hundred years, it is difficult to see how our economic system can be challenged. While it has produced amazing prosperity for some, it has failed to lift millions from a life of misery.

As poor countries cannot meet the demands of their people, these countries face growing protests, conflicts, and civil wars. These, together with the effects of climate change, have encouraged refugees and migrants in growing numbers to seek entrance into nations where they can live in some safety and well-being. At the same time richer nations find themselves increasingly unable to deal with refugees, climate change, and violent crime caused by rising inequality. Migrants and refugees around the world are eroding the concept of *nation*. Those desperate to hold on to their racial and nationalistic identity are threatened by what they see as the replacement of their kind of people and their values. This too has fed the so-called culture wars in the United States and Western Europe.

Complicating things further is the threat of a global war. The war in Ukraine seemed almost unreal in the twenty-first century until the world realized that it might just be the precursor to a greater conflict. Most nations are now increasing their armaments. NATO is expanding. Germany and Japan are doubling their military spending. China threatens to invade Taiwan. Already the war in Ukraine has not only devastated a nation but has threatened the world's energy and food supply. Israel is attacked by Hamas and Gaza is decimated.

Historically global wars for the past five hundred years have occurred about once every hundred years. The last two were the Napoleonic Wars (1803–1815) and the German Wars (1914–1945), often called World Wars I and II. Global wars are distinctively different from other conflicts because battles take place around the world with an excessive number of casualties. They are also unique because they are about the leadership of the entire global system.[5] The United States emerged from World War II as the prime victor and was able to set the rules and institutions for the international agenda for a century. Those rules and agenda are now being challenged by Russia and China. This makes the threat of another global conflict much more likely.

The world may be at the brink of a global transition or system shift from our present system to something else. The world has experienced such worldwide system changes before, as when Rome fell. This ended the imperial system that had lasted since the Assyrian Empire in 721 BC. It

---

5. Modelski, *Long Cycles in World Politics*, 39–46.

also signaled the beginning of the Middle Ages and feudalism. Another system shift occurred with the emergence of capitalism and the nation-state system from feudalism five hundred years ago. These transitions were not easy and caused widespread devastation and destruction, which we may be beginning to experience again.

GROWING FEARS

Sitting down to a good meal and watching numerous advertisements for the good life, most people in richer nations, and even the well-to-do in poor nations, can put off worrying about a sharp change to their lifestyle. Yet, as screens overflow with drought and floods, worry manages to creep in. Gun violence happens nearby. Nothing seems to get done in the nation's capital. The mail brings appeals to help starving children. Thousands more cross the border. Russia mentions a nuclear option and North Korea sends off another intercontinental missile.

There is no panic, but numbness sets in because we cannot do anything about the troubles all around. The problems are too many and the solutions are too far away. While adults, busy as usual, cope by doing their everyday tasks, it is tougher on the young. Some, set back by the pandemic, find it so hard to keep up with assignments. Others, depressed by climate change ruining their future, wonder if hard work is worth it. A global survey revealed that young people across the world are depressed over the planet's future.[6] Young people make up most migrants and refugees. They are also those most at risk in protests, civil conflicts, and, if it comes to that, a world war. Making everything worse is the blame game. Problems are seen as being caused by the other side and solutions are viewed as unworkable if they are proposed by the opposition. Divisions have always been with us but now the stakes are higher.

CAN CHURCHES HELP?

At this time, churches are ill equipped to deal with the coming crises. In America young people are leaving the churches and rethinking their faith.[7] They are joining an increasing number of people who, when asked about

---

6. Hickman et al., "Climate Anxiety in Children."
7. Kinnaman, *You Lost Me.*

Introduction

their church affiliation, answer "None." A whole body of literature has risen about these "Nones" who have left the church or never belonged.[8] Fewer students are also preparing to be pastors. There has been a 43 percent decline in the past ten years for those enrolling in a Master of Divinity degree.[9] Church attendance has fallen to 85 percent of what it was before the pandemic. More churches are selling their property. 4,500 churches closed in 2019 while only 3,000 new churches were born.[10]

The vulnerability of the churches has made them concentrate on their own survival and growth. Appeals for evangelism follow descriptions of church loss and are often motivated by the need to keep the institution going. The financial weakness of congregations and denominations also makes them timid in addressing societal issues. Even Pope Francis was criticized for his defense of refugees and indictment of European populism. His opponents were quick to point out that his stand could bring down the physical and financial apparatus of the Catholic Church.[11]

In the Global South, Christian churches are burgeoning but, at the same time, many of their members struggle for the necessities of life. Climate change is affecting undeveloped nations faster than elsewhere. Though many Christians there cry out for fairness and justice, they are far removed from those who could erase their nation's debt or employ the thousands of young people entering the work force. Though people might back one candidate over another at election time, it will not change the fact that they live in a poor country.

THE ECLIPSE OF THE KINGDOM

In good times and bad, the institutional church became the bellwether of the Christian message. For many, the vitality and relevance of the faith rested on the growth or decline of church attendance. In the process, the Kingdom of God, the chief subject of Jesus' ministry, and indeed of the entire Scriptures, has been pushed aside. This is because the Kingdom has been eclipsed in theology and church life. Though it is the most important concept in Gospels and the Scriptures as a whole, the Kingdom of God has almost lost its relevance to the problems of this world. One reason was that

8. White, *Rise of the Nones*; and Barna and Kinnaman, *Churchless*.
9. Post, "Theological Schools Report."
10. Gabbert, "Losing Their Religion."
11. Engle and Werner, "Steve Bannon and U.S Ultra-Conservatives."

the Kingdom has been defined as an eschatological event or a reference to the coming of the Kingdom in the end times. This position was put forward through the work of Johannes Weiss and Albert Schweitzer.[12] Their concerns were echoed by many theologians and churchmen in the following years.[13] The eclipse of the Kingdom's significance to this world was also the result of a literal reading of Matthew's terminology of the "Kingdom of Heaven." Even though Matthew used the word "heaven" instead of "God" because of the Jewish fear of using God's name in vain, many of the faithful simply thought of the Kingdom as the path to heaven.

The importance of the Kingdom to the problems of this world has been reasserted again. While acknowledging that the Kingdom is ultimately focused on the world to come, C. H. Dodd stated that the future Kingdom was also partially "realized" in this realm.[14] In his classic study *The Kingdom of God*, John Bright found that the Kingdom is the unifying theme of the whole Bible.[15] More recently N. T. Wright in his several works has argued that the Kingdom be brought to the fore in church life as it was at the time of Christ.[16] Perhaps even more significant is that biblical scholars are looking more closely at the social conditions at the time of the biblical documents. This helps to understand the issues they addressed and how their message was received. In Old Testament studies George Mendenhall and Norman Gottwald have underscored how the faith of Israel was diametrically opposed to the economic and political systems of Egypt and Canaan.[17]

In New Testament studies, more attention is being given to the social conditions of the world at the time of Christ. This helps to illuminate the significance of Christ's teaching and its impact on society. Helmut Koester explores the history, culture, and religion of the Hellenistic age as part of his introduction to the New Testament. He illuminates the lives of slaves, the position of women, and the economics of empire.[18] As we see the thrust of the biblical teachings of the Kingdom on the societies of both the Old

---

12. Weiss, *Jesus' Proclamation of the Kingdom*; and Schweitzer, *Quest of the Historical Jesus*.

13. Perrin, *Kingdom of God*, 56–57.

14. Dodd, *Parables of the Kingdom*, 35.

15. Bright, *Kingdom of God*, 7.

16. Wright, *Simply Jesus* and *How God Became King*.

17. Gottwald, *Tribes of Israel*, 642–49; and Mendenhall, *Tenth Generation*, 194–97.

18. Koester, *History, Culture, and Religion*.

Introduction

and New Testaments, it empowers us to do the same for our contemporary world.

Can this rediscovery of the Kingdom bring hope in a world undergoing profound changes and possible system shift? As Pastor Mike writes his sermon on the "good news" of the kingdom to a dwindling congregation, and Pastor Kansa prepares to address those whose very lives are threatened, is Jesus' announcement of the nearness of the Kingdom "good news" today?

RECAPTURING THE FOCUS ON THE KINGDOM

The chief purpose of this book is to bring the good news of the Kingdom of God to a whole generation leaving the church and to those struggling to keep the church from closing. *The Kingdom of God is God's fulfillment of the promises of the prophets, which are partially realized in this life, providing hope for this world, and will find their perfect completion in the life to come.* Here the Kingdom is not defined as the *reign of God* but rather as the *providence of God*. It is not based chiefly upon human effort but upon Christ working in history. It is not restricted to what the church can accomplish. It is rather what Christ is accomplishing through all institutions and all people he has made to bring about a greater realization of the promises of the Kingdom.

To bring the good news of the Kingdom to those of us who are frankly worried about what is happening to our world, the church should again elevate the Kingdom of God as the focus of the Christian faith and mission. Christ was far more concerned about the Kingdom than he was about attendance at the synagogue or the leadership of the Sanhedrin. The Kingdom was the subject of his message. The Kingdom provided the curriculum for the theological education of the disciples. In a deeply polarized, enemy-occupied nation, he challenged people to believe "good news" and began to bring it about. Carl Braaten writes, "The gospel of the Kingdom of God can be taken as the most adequate starting point for the mission of the church."[19]

To lift up the Kingdom of God as the focal point of the Christian faith and its mission is a daunting task. The kids of Pastor Mike and Pastor Kansa and their generation are not likely to discover on their own the Kingdom's treasure hidden in the field or the pearl of great price (Matt 13:44–46). The secrets of the Kingdom do not come to mind naturally when confronted by disaster (Mark 4:11). Even after the disciples had been with Jesus for three

---

19. Braaten, *Flaming Center*, 42.

years, they still did not fully understand what the Kingdom was all about (Acts 1:6).

This book is written for pastors, seminary students, and generations of young and old people seeking hope and joy in a scary world. It is not escapist because it confronts the world as it is and not as we would like it to be. Nor does it provide a simplistic antidote. Instead, it wrestles with the biblical hope in dire circumstances and does so joyfully, confident that as Christ announced the nearness of the Kingdom, he is working to see it happen.

THE GOOD NEWS

The aim of this book is to show how Christ's Kingdom is coming among us. The nearness of Christ's Kingdom brings with it the need to repent and also the courage to hope. First it searches the Scriptures to identify the blessings of the Kingdom in the midst grave challenges. The Scriptures also identify the Kingdom as the chief purpose of the church's mission. Second, it looks to history to see how the vision of the Kingdom addressed the crises they faced and shaped the culture and politics of their day. It also shows us how the Kingdom can address challenges in our world. Third, it gives us hope by recognizing a worldwide network of people through whom Christ is working. We are not alone in bringing the blessings of the Kingdom to the most vulnerable. Even in conditions of bad government, Kingdom workers help to heal, build consensus, and dream of a better future. Last of all, the book points out how many more people can be involved in the ministry of the church, and how they can bring the good news of the Kingdom to others.

THE KINGDOM POINTS THE WAY

To discover how the Kingdom produces hope in a grim world, we will mine the Scriptures for their treasures. The Bible tells stories of how God gets people through some unbelievable trials. At the very beginning, when God was King, God delivered a whole people from slavery. YHWH was their God, and they would be his people. God fed them, gave them water to drink, forgave them, healed them, and saved them from death. These were the blessings of God's kingship. But when God was rejected as King, and the covenant laws were flouted, the rich stole from the poor and sex was used for profit. The prophets and Jesus called for repentance then and

INTRODUCTION

continue to do so today. Without a change in our culture, our politics, and our corporations, devastation awaits us now as it did before the destruction of Samaria and Judea.

But the prophets also promised a renewal of God's blessings. Sins would be forgiven, the hungry would be fed, water would appear in the wilderness, the sick and lame would be healed, homes and incomes would be restored, slaves and prisoners would be liberated, there would be peace between nations and an end to death. These promises provided not only hope but also a sense of identity.

When Jesus proclaimed that the Kingdom was near, it was met with disbelief. Then Jesus healed, fed, forgave, warned the rich, raised he dead, and complemented the enemy for his faith. Despite these signs of the Kingdom, Jesus was crucified as a fraudulent king. But in the resurrection hope was reborn. The Kingdom was not limited to what happened on earth. The perfect fulfillment of the promises of the prophets was now guaranteed. Meanwhile, Jesus talked about the ethics of the Kingdom and their primacy over all other ethics by saying that the final judgement on our faithfulness will be whether we have fed the hungry, given water to the thirsty, clothed the poor, visited the sick and imprisoned, and befriended refugees (Matt 25:31–46).

After the ascension the good news of the Kingdom could not be repressed. Forgiveness was preached to thousands, hungry people were fed, prisoners were released, the lame leaped, political enemies were baptized, and the dead were raised. The message quickly spread, centered in the cross and resurrection, forgiveness and eternal life. But collection for the poor in distant Jerusalem had high priority. In the final pages of Acts Luke writes, "He [Paul] lived there two whole years . . . proclaiming the Kingdom of God and teaching about the Lord Jesus Christ" (Acts 28:30–31).

THE KINGDOM ADVANCES CIVILIZATION

With the destruction of the Roman Empire the church provided a tenuous sense of unity for the Middle Ages. Augustine addressed the crisis in *The City of God*, which he identified with the Kingdom of God.[20] With the Scriptures he pointed out a path through the unknown perils of the future. Addressing another monumental system shift from the end of feudalism and the beginning of the nation-state system, Luther also spoke of the

---

20. Augustine, *City of God*, 514.

Kingdom. Freeing the state from churchly rule and freeing the church to concentrate on communicating the graciousness of God, he divided the Kingdom into the two ways God works in the world.[21] The political insights of Augustine and Luther, inspired by their views of the Kingdom of God, have helped to influence the ways faith and polity interact in our world.

In the last five hundred years capitalism and the nation-state system have presented new problems. Once again, people moved by the promises of the Kingdom, or simply seeking a better life, have brought about significant change for the better. Colonialism was challenged, slavery was ended, billions were saved from starvation, wars have been prevented, and Christ's forgiveness and the hope of eternal life have been spread across the world. Now the Kingdom can address the problems of world inequality, climate change, failed states, and refugees. Jesus still calls for repentance; more challenging still, he calls for the faith to believe that blessings are on their way.

THE KINGDOM'S WORLDWIDE NETWORK GENERATES HOPE

One way to communicate the promises of the Kingdom to our current crises might be to rename the Kingdom "God's New World Society." From all over the world people have come together to promote the United Nations' millennial goals. Advocates from churches, world religions, nongovernmental organizations, and political leaders are together promoting many Kingdom aims. As Christians work together with them, there will be good opportunities to share the special Kingdom goals of Christ's offer of forgiveness and the hope of the resurrection.

As the world faces new and dangerous problems, we are presented with the choice of dealing with them either through coercive authoritarian regimes or through consensual, more democratic ones. Given the tremendous differences between rich nations and poor, could a system be designed to move into a more consensual, democratic system on a world scale? Politically, such a system might be described as "soft" power manifested as a new world culture aimed at bringing the benefits of the Kingdom to the most vulnerable.

To be effective, such a new world culture needs to break through the numbness we currently experience. In the Scriptures the prophets attacked

---

21. Bornkamm, *Luther's Doctrine of the Two Kingdoms*, 8.

that numbness with warnings of catastrophe and then the amazing vision of what might be and what will be. It brought energy and hope to fearful and depressed people. Now a social scientist is calling for "utopistics."[22] This is the ambitious description of a better world and employing social science to help bring it about.

AN EXILED CHURCH EXPANDS ITS MINISTRY

It is a sad day when a church closes because it can no longer afford a pastor or there are no funds to plant a new church. In the Babylonian exile God's people created new patterns of worship and devotion. When Jesus' disciples were exiled from the temple and synagogues, elders were blessed to share the word, baptize, and commune the faithful. Money was not necessary to be the church. If the Kingdom of God, "God's New World Society," can be the focus of the Christian faith and mission, people can concentrate on Kingdom goals. If the church is not dependent on funds for its buildings and personnel, larger collections can again be for the poor and the unity of the churches across the world (1 Cor 16:1–4).

In the approaching tectonic shift in the world system, young people will suffer the most. They will have to spend their lives dealing with the climate and environment. They are the most likely to become immigrants crossing seas and borders. They will be called upon to fight wars and suffer most from post-traumatic stress disorder. They are the ones most likely to suffer the hate and depression of a polarized society. It is to this generation that the words of Jesus are most powerful. "[T]he Kingdom of God has come near; repent, and believe in the good news" (Mark 1:15). This was wonderful news at that time. As we find ways to say it and live it, it will bring new hope to the young and others.

THE LAST KINGDOM STANDING

Nebuchadnezzar had a nightmare. He dreamt of a marvelous statue of gold, bronze, and iron but with feet of iron and clay. The prophet Daniel said it represented empires, one following another, until at the end it rested upon the feet, an unstable mixed combination of iron and clay. Then a stone, not cut by human hands, hit the feet, and the statue collapsed. The fall of the

---

22. Wallerstein, *End of the World*, 217.

statue, representing the fall of empires, ushered in the Kingdom of God, which would fill all the earth (Dan 2:1–39). The collapse of those feet of iron and clay might also be a stunning illustration of the end the world as we know it. Yet, the promise of the Kingdom of God brings new hope to all of us, particularly the young. Out of the rubble God has been building a new Kingdom. He has compassion for the vulnerable people around us. These are the masses of unemployed youth around the world who have no future. They are the refugees by the millions. They are the innocent victims of rape as militants stalk Africa for its gold and diamonds. They are citizens of Ukraine shot down in the streets, and those massacred in the Israel/Gaza war. As nations fail and the economic system cannot provide for the most vulnerable, God promises a better Kingdom. Jesus announced that the Kingdom was near. Though other kingdoms will come to an end, God's Kingdom will remain *The Last Kingdom Standing*.

Chapter 1

When God Was King

Yes, there is a path through the crises of ecological disaster, raging inequality, the threat of a world war, increasing authoritarianism, failed states, refugees, and the end of the world as we know it. It is the Kingdom of God announced by Jesus. How might the Kingdom of God be best described? During Israel's tribal alliance, described from Exodus to Judges, the Kingdom of God was a veritable cornucopia of gifts, and they were received without a central government, taxes, or a military draft.

THE KING AND LIBERATION

What was it like when God was King? In the midst of injustice, dislocation, famine, and conflict, God provided liberation and essentials for life. When God was King, slaves were liberated from Egypt. It was a miraculous event and was inscribed on God's covenant with Israel, the King's constitution: "I am the Lord your God, who brought you out of the land of Egypt" (Exod 20:2). That extraordinary series of events created the Jewish people, whose very existence is celebrated in the Passover Seder.

Liberated from an oppressive regime, how would a motley crowd of ex-slaves be formed into a new people that would not duplicate the tyranny of Pharoah's empire? How might it keep alive the liberation that formed the very essence of their identity? George Mendenhall describes the covenant at Sinai as a unique event. It was a break from the governance of coercive politics to the creation of a community based on common obligations rather than on shared interests—on ethics rather than covetousness.[1]

A significant part of those obligations would be about the treatment of slaves. The liberation of slaves was continued in Jewish moral law. Hebrew slaves were to be freed after seven years. If married, they would take their wives with them (Exod 20:2–4). Still, not all slavery was abolished. Slaves from another nation could remain the possession of their owners (Lev 25:46).

The remnants of slavery are still felt around the world, even to the point of the descendants of slaves demanding reparations from those who profited from it. Human trafficking, forced labor, and children working in slave-like conditions constitute contemporary slavery. Jails hold political prisoners who have demonstrated against corruption and illegitimate regimes.

Without prisons among a nomadic people, the penalties for crime were severe. Yet, when God was King six cities of refuge were created to harbor all those who injured or killed someone without intent (Num 35:10–28). They also served as a place of safety from vengeful relatives until a fair trial could be held. This not only provided liberation for the innocent, but also lessened the potential for long lasting blood feuds.

FOOD AND WATER

In a world where hunger still affects millions and mothers must walk miles for water, it is good to remember that when God was King the people were provided with food and water. At the time of extreme necessity, it began with the miraculous. In the desert God provided manna for all the people. Those who gathered much had nothing left over and those who gathered little had no shortage. Together with the manna, God provided meat from quails, which covered the camp. Provision of this manna lasted forty years before they entered the land of Canaan (Exod 16:4–35). But when the miraculous was no longer necessary, food could be purchased, perhaps with the treasures given to them from the Egyptians (Deut 2:6). With the same funds the people, no doubt, would have purchased animals for meat to sustain them in the wilderness. Their animals were also an important part of the sacrificial system centered in the tabernacle.

---

1. Mendenhall, *Ancient Israel's Faith*, 21–22.

After three days in the wilderness the people only found bitter water. God showed Moses a piece of wood. Throwing it into the water made the water sweet (Exod 5:22–25). After much complaining about the lack of water, God told Moses to strike a rock with his staff and water poured out for the people (Exod 17:1–6). At another time Moses was told to command water to come out of the rock, but he struck it with his staff instead. Even in his disobedience water came for all the people and their livestock (Num 20:2–10).

Concerning these events Gottwald writes, "The people had to learn to survive on a makeshift diet. Including quail blown in from the sea and a bread substitute of 'manna.' Water was a common deficiency, and apparently only as they found their way to the multiple springs around Kadesh were they able to establish a viable existence."[2] When the people were settled, water was still vital for life. God as King promised the early rain and the late rain that they might gather in their grain and wine and oil. Yet it was conditional, depending upon whether they remained faithful to God and his commands (Deut 11:14–17).

FORGIVING AND HEALING

Complaint against leaders is almost universal. When people criticized Moses for bringing them to the wilderness, they were tired of the "worthless" food and scarcity of water. Then the Lord sent poisonous serpents that bit the people so that many died and others were gravely ill. God told Moses to make a serpent and set it upon a pole so that all who gazed on it would live. In one act healing and forgiveness came together to save lives and conscience (Num 21:5–9). It was an exceptional event, but forgiveness and provisions for health were to become a regular part of the everyday life of the people.

Sacrifices for guilt and sin were at the heart of worship at the tabernacle. Some sins were unintentional; others were deliberate. Through sacrifices of animals, their sin and guilt were forgiven. In addition, the sins of the whole nation were absolved in the yearly Day of Atonement. The undeserved compassion of God for his people was enshrined in the ark of the covenant. There, made out of pure gold, was the mercy seat, the most important part of that shrine of the covenant.

---

2. Gottwald, *Tribes of Yahweh*, 455.

Provisions for health were also supplied in the extensive rules about sickness and cleanliness. In addition to conducting sacrifices, priests also served as public health officials. Looking back to that time from our contemporary world, everyday stress and mental health concerns were addressed through the laws of the Sabbath, where rest and recovery were built into the weekly schedule.

LAND FOR REFUGEES

When God was King, a good land was supplied for a nation of migrants. This land had flowing streams and underground waters. It was a land of wheat and barley, of vines and fig trees and pomegranates, olive trees and honey (Deut 8:7–8). In writing about the land they were about to enter, Brueggemann writes, "The yearning to belong somewhere, to have a home, to be in a safe place, is a deep and moving pursuit."[3] If this is a longing for strangers in a settled society, it is much greater for those who have had to leave their home, culture, and vocations in another civilization. For Israel, the culture shock from being a nomadic people to becoming farmers was enormous. Yet, by having a place to grow that provided them with food and security, the people had come home.

The gift of land began with the miraculous, with crossing the Jordan and the destruction of Jericho. The land was distributed to each tribe and to each family in a fair and equal manner. In the new land there was no private land ownership. The land belonged to God. War was not initiated in pursuit of land or slaves. All captured land belonged to God and the people could enjoy it and pass it down to their families if they remained faithful to the covenant law.[4] Leviticus 25 underscores God's ownership and the resulting limitations on property accumulation and slavery. While people could freely buy or sell land, in the fiftieth year the land was to be returned to those who had farmed it or their descendants. Slaves were released. If a brother was in difficulty, you were obligated to help and maintain them without charging any interest. This was a radical break from the Egypt that Moses knew too well. God was not governing by head-of-state triumphalism and the politics of oppression and exploitation. God was king of justice and compassion.[5] From a sociological viewpoint the real uniqueness

---

3. Brueggemann, *Land*, 1.
4. Mendenhall, *Ancient Israel's Faith*, 91.
5. Brueggemann, *Prophetic Imagination*, 6.

of Israel was its egalitarian social system in the middle of vertically stratified societies. This enabled it to function reasonably well in the Palestinian highlands for centuries.[6]

AN UNEVEN PEACE

After Jericho, God promised to be with the people and help them in their conquests. The battle for the land continued with fits and starts using conventional strategy and wisdom. There was no clear victory or lasting peace. For many, it was not clear who was the enemy. Instead of defeating the Canaanites for their immoral practices and decadent behavior, many Israelites joined them. Then God no longer supported them in battle. "Whenever they marched out, the hand of the Lord was against them to bring misfortune as the Lord had warned them" (Judg. 2:15).

Nevertheless, God raised up judges who delivered the people from the enemies that plundered them. With no standing army, judges like Ehud, Deborah, Gideon, and others fought singly and with volunteer militia to protect the settlers and bring about an uneven peace. However, more problems appeared on the horizon. If the people were so influenced by the religion of their neighbors, would the rich observe the Year of Jubilee in Leviticus 25 and the other laws that shared the wealth of the community? If not, would the common people willingly volunteer to protect the wealth of the unjust? Coupled with the threats of the Philistines on the coast with their chariots, the elders asked for a king.

REJECTING GOD'S KINGSHIP

When Samuel, the last of the judges, became old, all the elders of Israel came together to ask for a king. The stated reason was that Samuel's sons were corrupt. But behind their demand was the history of attacks from their neighbors and war among the tribes themselves. On the coast the Philistines presented a sinister new threat. Israel's enemies had kings, central governments, and standing armies. Just to defend themselves and bring unity to the tribes, Israel thought it needed a king as well.

Samuel resisted the idea. Not only was it a personal affront but it had big implications. He prayed to God and God answered, "Listen to the voice

---

6. Gottwald, *Tribes of Yahweh*, 692–93.

of the people in all they say to you, for they have not rejected you, but *they have rejected me from being King over them*" (1 Sam 8:7). This was nothing new; God had been ignored and denied before. If they wanted a king, Samuel should grant their demand. However, he should warn them and show them the ways of a king who would reign over them. It would be different, and worse, than when God had been their king.

The most important parts of God's kingship were the gifts of freedom from slavery and oppression. Then there were the gifts of food and drink, forgiveness, and healing. Then God gave them the prosperous land, flowing with milk and honey. Yes, he also gave them laws for rest, for health, for order, and for security. Above all, God ordered society for the benefit of the most vulnerable and the least advantaged. Israel had laws but they always followed God's gifts. This is an alternate understanding of the Kingdom of God to the one that is often given. Seeking to better communicate to a modern audience, some who view the Kingdom in this way have called the Kingdom the "Reign of God."[7]

With that terminology the emphasis is on God's sovereignty over the nations.[8] It speaks about God's power. When God was King in the tribal confederacy, God's power, commands, and punishments for sin were seen to predominate. This period of Israel's history is sometimes called a theocracy. In modern theocracies, the city of the Vatican, Iran, or Taliban enforce laws they believe come from God. But the occasional judges of Israel, emerging from the people in no regular order, were quite unlike modern theocracies.

THE KINGSHIP OF GOD

The story of God's kingship has three lessons for all seeking God's aid. The first is that miracles are for emergencies. The slaves walk through the water to freedom. Hunger is averted; thirst is quenched. Just looking at the raised serpent is the cure. But when the emergency is over, God brings blessings through laws, mutual help, and the provisions of nature.

The second lesson is that the good results are only partial, never quite complete. To have tastier food the freed slaves wanted to go back to their masters. People got tired of the life-giving manna. There was simply not enough water. Many died of snake bite. Despite God's overwhelming gifts

---

7. Arias, *Announcing the Reign of God*, and Hilkert and Schreiter, *Praxis of the Reign of God*.

8. Perrin, *Kingdom of God*, 44–46.

in freeing an oppressed people, nourishing them, and bringing them to a prosperous land, many of them worshipped other gods and ignored the practices that would guarantee a better life for all.

The third lesson is that God as King works slowly. It took ten plagues to change Pharoah's mind. Then it took forty years in the wilderness to create the sense of a nation under God. The conquest of the land was never fully accomplished until the time of David, five hundred years later. More important was that despite the impatience of people and their complaints, God continued to forgive, bless, and push people to fulfill the goals God had for them. These lessons from the time when God was King are important because they are often repeated throughout the Scriptures.

ROOTS OF DEMOCRACY

Today, at a critical juncture of world history, people around the world are debating the merits of democracy versus authoritarian government. Bringing this into sharp focus are the wars in Ukraine and Gaza. Then there is the threat of the invasion of Taiwan by China. This brings into sharp contrast the autocratic regimes of Russia and China with the relatively democratic nations of Ukraine and Taiwan. The conflict between democracy and authoritarian rule was also demonstrated in the assault on the US capital by people seeking to overthrow the election of the US president. Do the Scriptures have anything to say on the subject?

The kings of Israel were certainly not democratic, nor were the Assyrians or Babylonians who conquered Samaria and Judea. The Roman Empire, even with some indirect rule, could not be considered democratic. The tribal confederacy, when God was King, was the closest thing to democracy in the Bible. Early Israel was not like its neighbors with a vertical organization with a single governor or king. Rather, it was a confederation of tribes. Their unity was not based on race or nationality but rather on a covenant with Yahweh. They were to be a "priestly kingdom and a holy nation" (Exod 19:6). This was their constitution, but there was no political institution to enforce it. There was no statehood, no central government, and no administration. Instead, the ark of the covenant at Shiloh united their devotion and unified the community.[9] The confederation was also strengthened through three annual feasts: that of the unleavened bread

---

9. Bright, *History of Israel*, 143.

(Passover), the picking the first fruits, and the ingathering of the harvest at the end of the year (Exod 23:16).

One of the democratic roots of the people of Israel was in the initial covenant constitution. It was made with all the people when God promised, "I will take you as my people, and I will be your God" (Exod 6:7). It was a dramatic contrast to the covenants of the Canaanitic cities. Covenants were also made with the gods of those cities, but they were made not with the people but instead with the king.[10] Thus, the king would receive the special favor of God in his rule, but the people were the subjects, not of God but of their king.

Another feature of the tribal confederacy were laws promoting economic justice by prohibiting interest, releasing slaves, abolishing debt, and enacting provisions for land reform (Lev 25). These almost would be considered communist today. Yet, the vital difference between these and state communism, as has been practiced by governments, was that there was no central administration or (king) to enforce these provisions. This may be the reason that there is no evidence in the Scriptures that they were ever observed. Nonetheless, as we shall see, they provided the rationale for the prophets castigating the rich and Jesus' warning of wealth.

The fact that the tribal confederacy, when God was King, ultimately ended contains a warning for all democracies. If the provisions for economic justice are not observed, it is not likely that the poor people of a society have enough loyalty to the society to defend it and see it survive. Apparently, the elders of Israel were afraid that volunteer militias could not be counted on to defend the people. Cracks can be seen in modern democracies when the poor are lined up for food and when gun violence takes lives in poverty-stricken neighborhoods. When the wealthy can buy politicians through political contributions, is it truly a *democracy* of the people, by the people, and for the people?

LIMITED GOVERNMENT

Without a king, a central government, and an administrative bureaucracy, the tribal confederacy had a limited government. As such, it would seem to be a model for those in the United States and other democracies who advocate a smaller role for government. Yet, that limited government could only work if there were economic justice with land reform, curbs against

---

10. Noll, "Canaanitic Religion."

exploitation, and simple fairness. Under those conditions people will volunteer to protect and defend that type of society.

Tragically, those advocating a more limited government today are often those supported by the wealthy. In the modern context, calls for "limited government" are often objections to the government working to protect the most vulnerable in society, those left by the wayside in a capitalist economy. Efforts to protect the most vulnerable, however, are in line with the Kingdom of God as outlined in Leviticus 25. Modern calls, then, are rejections of the ideals of God's kingship, just as the elders' demand for a king over Israel at the end of the tribal confederacy was a rejection of the idea that God was King.

For many, Samuel's objections to a king might seem to be like the pique of an old-fashioned guy who has not kept up with the times. Yet, as we shall see, his convictions are echoed throughout the history of Israel, the ministry of Jesus, and the political role of God's people in the coming transitions.

Chapter 2

Politics on Trial

WE OFTEN LOOK TO politics to achieve a moral purpose such as staying safe, getting jobs, enjoying prosperity, having shelter, aiding the poor, and having access to education. But to obtain and retain power people in politics often must make compromises that impede their ability to achieve moral goals. Nonetheless, the largest moral issues of the age are contested in politics. Aid organizations pressure governments to do more to help the poor. Abortion rights have moved from being a religious issue to a political one. How women dress is a political issue in Muslim nations. Authoritarian governments suppress the freedom of the press. Fears for security argue for more defense spending.

As moral issues become politicized, whole societies are polarized into what have come to be called "culture wars." Disputes that used to be argued within the realm of religion are now weaponized for political gain. In the United States white evangelicals unite against abortion, homosexuality, and pornography. They are supported by a group of wealthy, well-connected businessmen who encouraged pastors to decry the evils of socialism and extol the virtues of capitalism. Eighty-one percent of white evangelicals voted for Trump in 2016.[1] Near the same time that this group became more politicized, an increasing number of moderates left the churches and became the so-called "Nones," who claim no church affiliation.[2] Then, to exercise their moral concerns, those leaving the churches got more involved in politics to counter the political demands of the evangelical right.

1. Burge, *Nones*, 50–51.
2. Burge, *Nones*, 66.

THE PROBLEM WITH POLITICS

After the elders of Israel demanded a king, Samuel warned them of what would happen. As the king would need soldiers, there would be a draft. Virtuous daughters would become courtesans working as perfumers and cooks. Their God-given land would be taken and given to the backers of the king. What once were offerings to God now would become imposed taxes for the government. The king would commandeer their slaves, and, in the end, even make their owners his slaves (1 Sam 8:11–17).

Despite the warnings, the people replied that they were determined to have a king over them. God would no longer be their King. Now it would be questionable whether his laws for health, for sex, and for worship would be observed. In effect, God would still be God, but would be kicked upstairs just to do divine things. In the nitty-gritty things of the world, they wanted a king they could see, honor, and obey. They demanded to be like the other nations around them, with a strong vertical command structure headed by a king.

God had heard enough and reluctantly told Samuel to give them a king. The words in Deuteronomy had come to pass. "When you have come into the land that the LORD your God is giving you and have taken possession of it and settled in it, and you say, 'I will set a king over me, like all the nations that are around me, you may indeed set over you a king whom the LORD your God will choose" (Deut 17:14–15). In politics appearance is everything and good looks are invaluable. Samuel was led to the tallest, best-looking man in the land named Saul and anointed him as king. Then in an assembly of all the tribes lots were drawn for new king. Repeated lots for tribe, clan, family, and finally person were cast, and Saul was acknowledged as king by the people. A call for help came to Saul soon after. The Ammonites threatened to take out the right eyes of everyone they conquered. In dramatic fashion Saul recruited three hundred thousand men, defeated the Ammonites, and brought joy to the people, who gladly accepted Saul as king (1 Sam 9–11).

To be successful and to retain power in politics, it is sometimes necessary to cut corners and do immoral things to accomplish other "moral" objectives. Confronted with the Philistine army with thirty thousand chariots and six thousand horsemen, Israelites began to desert their posts. Instead of trusting the Lord for victory, Saul sought to rally the troops with sacrifices he was not to perform. For this disobedience God turned against Saul and told him that his kingdom would not continue. Instead, God would search out another after his own heart to be the next ruler (1 Sam 13:2–14). He and his son Jonathan were soon to die in battle.

Like Saul, politicians are tempted to forsake some of their convictions to stay in power. Some lie; others abandon their principles to raise money for their next election. Because it happens so often, it brings politics into disrepute. "That's politics" is a way of dismissing politicians and their activities from the world of common sense and moral purpose. Despite the almost universal recognition that politicians need to behave this way to gain and retain power, it is ironic that we trust the political system to decide our most heartfelt ethical issues. Sometimes, however, politics and righteousness can come closer together.

THE KINGDOM OF DAVID

The Star of David is on Israel's flag today. David is remembered and honored as Israel's best king. He centralized the government in Jerusalem. He extended the boundaries of Israel and for the first time brought all the remnants of the Canaanites under his rule. Samuel's warnings had come true. Now there were professional soldiers, a draft, taxes, and palace adultery. Yet, David's attitudes and policies reflected some of the moral values of the tribal league confederacy when God was King.

His personal devotion to God was exemplary. He rejoiced in securing the ark of the covenant with its mercy seat (2 Sam 6:12–17). He desired to build a temple to God but was told that would be the task of his son. Though there is no record of practicing the Year of Jubilee under his reign, David's Psalms are filled with his concern for the poor. He writes, "For the needy shall not always be forgotten, nor the hope of the poor perish forever" (Ps 9:18). He commends those who help the poor when he sings, "Happy are those who consider the poor; the LORD delivers them in the day of trouble. The LORD protects them and keeps them alive; they are called happy in the land" (Ps 41:1). Other references and concerns for the poor are found throughout the Psalms.

Quite dramatically, forgiveness is prominent in David's reign. He was both forgiven and forgiving. In his adultery with Bathsheba and murder of her husband, he is excoriated by the prophet and his son by Bathsheba dies. Yet despite his crimes he prayed for forgiveness: "Have mercy on me, O God, according to your steadfast love; according to your abundant mercy blot out my transgressions" (Ps 51:1). Despite his son Absalom's move to take over the whole kingdom from his father, David mourned his son's death and said, "Would that I had died instead of you" (2 Sam 18:33). Though David punished many of Saul's descendants out of concern that they would rise against him, he had mercy on some like Mephibosheth, the son of Jonathan (1 Sam 9:10–13).

At the end of David's reign, the nation was mostly at peace despite some continuing domestic threats to his rule and a few attacks from the Philistines. Nevertheless, it had only been achieved by bloodshed. Because of the blood on his hands, David was not to build the temple. David's legacy was not to be in the cedar and stone of the temple but rather in the memory of his kingship. From that time on the hopes and dreams of Israel, and later of Christians, would revolve around the coming of an even better King, descended from David. Yes, he was to be born in Bethlehem, in the city of David (Mic 5:2).

THE TEMPTATIONS OF POWER

How could a wise man be so foolish? That is the riddle of David's son Solomon. On becoming king, Solomon asks God for wisdom, which is freely given. Solomon makes a brilliant decision in a case brought to him. Thereafter fame of his wisdom is spread across the land and in neighboring nations. Using his wisdom, he also expands the kingdom and keeps the peace not through war but with alliances through marriage and diplomacy. In a massive effort he builds the exquisite temple to God. Brueggemann remarks on one troubling significance of the temple when he writes, "YHWH is now cornered in the temple. His business is to support of the regime, to grant legitimacy to it and to effect forgiveness when necessary."[3] Solomon then spends even more time building his palace.

To the casual observer, never had Israel enjoyed such security and prosperity. One might ask whether even modern Israel has achieved anything better. Throughout history the kingdom of David and Solomon has been the high point of Israel's political existence. That kingdom remained the ideal in the memories and longings of the Jewish people and their friends. Yet, much had been lost. Little remained of the tribal league including its provisions for the vulnerable. Now there were princes, but citizens were

---

3. Brueggemann, *Land*, 86.

often under their yoke. The state supported religion and religion placed itself in service to the state.[4] All seemed well, and then it all went wrong.

In his marriage alliances Solomon built worship places for his foreign wives and participated in their worship. In his building programs he used the forced labor of his subjects, fulfilling Samuel's warning that a king would use his people as slaves. To increase and maintain their power, politicians are tempted to do what is wrong. Power itself gives people the excuse to break the rules simply because they can, and they are not accountable to any immediate superior.

After the death of Solomon, God split the kingdom. Ahijah, a prophet of God, met Jeroboam, an able young man, and promised that he would be the leader of ten tribes of Israel that would no longer be loyal to the house of David. The capital of the new nation would be Samaria. Soon Jeroboam was faced with the dilemma that his people would be tempted to worship in Jerusalem. For political reasons, Jeroboam beguiled his people, ensnaring them to worship false gods and idols so that they might remain loyal to their government.[5] Once again religion was used to help prop up the government.

In succeeding years, the policies of the kings of Israel and Judah were profoundly influenced by the culture of their surrounding nations. Hard power was exercised through the king and his supporters in a vertical relationship. The survival of the state took precedence over their example to all nations under Yahweh, who created all people. Prosperity for the elite was the goal of the state even though it was built on the oppression of the poor.[6] Influenced both by the descendants of the Canaanites in their midst and the religion of their neighbors, both nations adopted the beliefs and practices of Baal worship. While to modern readers the difference between the worshippers of Yahweh and Ba'al might seem to be a denominational skirmish, the religions were diametrically opposed. Obedience to Yahweh summoned Israel to a life of goodness and fairness. Worship of Baal and his consort was a fertility faith that fostered people's animalistic nature and orgiastic practices for the purpose of gaining wealth.[7]

---

4. Bright, *Kingdom of God*, 39–41.

5. Augustine, *City of God*, 548.

6. This can be seen from the many references to the misery of the poor in the writings of Amos, Isaiah, and Jeremiah.

7. Bright, *Kingdom of God*, 51–52.

THE PROPHETIC RESTORATION

With the monarchy and politics, all of Samuel's warnings had come to pass. Given that, with a few exceptions, all the kings of Israel and Judah were evil, how might the worship of the one, universal God and the radical justice of the covenant be restored? It took place through the prophets. After the monarchy was begun, they were a political force that operated outside of the vertical power structure. The prophet Nathan brought God's message to David so that he repented (2 Sam 12:13). Elijah faced off with the prophets of Baal as a challenge to King Ahab and Jezebel, his wife (1 Kgs 18:20–40). Elisha, through a young companion, anointed Jehu to overthrow the dynasty of Ahab and to cause the death of Jezebel (2 Kgs 9:1–3).

The prophets not only had a hand in kingly rule, but they also did what kings could not. They healed people. Elijah revived a widow's son (1 Kgs 17:17–22). Reflecting a broader concern than that of his nation, Elisha healed Naaman, the commander of the Syrian army (2 Kgs 5:1–15). The prophets miraculously fed people (2 Kgs 4:42–44). They helped to bring victory to the nation by establishing a little peace (2 Kgs 3:1–27). Indeed, Elisha even raised one from the dead (2 Kgs 4:32–36).

Through their words and actions, the prophets kept alive the blessings of the covenant when God was King. In the monarchy God had become domesticated, worshipped in the new temple, and accessible to the king and his courtiers. For the kings of Israel, God was "on call," ready to be summoned when needed by the nation and its ruler.[8] But for the prophets the God of the covenant was the creator of all, unpredictable but compassionate. God was the friend of the hungry, the sick, and the helpless. Though kings counted on divine support in their efforts, many times God turned against them for the sake of justice.

THE CHANTING PROPHETS

Almost like contemporary rappers, the later prophets were anguished singers. Their messages were chiefly in poetry. Expressed in couplets, repeating a thought two times so that people would get it, the prophets sang. In the narrative of politics as usual, a certain numbness sets in. Crime continues; drought and floods get worse. The claims of rulers and the opposition are predictable. The struggle for power is a given. High moral tone is often the

---

8. Brueggemann, *Prophetic Imagination*, 28–29.

disguise for base motives. Regimes make grandiose claims of longevity and power, for example, Hitler foretelling a thousand-year Reich. But absent from the dominant narrative is grief and death. But this was not true of the prophetic chanters. Their task was and is to reveal the underlying truth that the pretense of the state is largely a façade.

The prophets do not scold or whine. Instead, they grieve over the death of the nation. It is in mourning that the prophets exercise their most telling criticism. The prophets walk together with the people to their common funeral. "They signal the collapse of our self-centeredness of the fearful practice of eating off the table of a hungry brother or sister." Those of all political stripes are in the procession to the grave. The vaunted claim that "doing it our way" will lead to continuing safety and prosperity is shown to be a political fantasy.[9]

For those who think that hard politics can fix it, the prophets bring forth the vision of the failed city-states of Samaria and Jerusalem. Contemporaries from modern-day Haiti would recognize that tragedy as their president was assassinated and gangs took over the country. Somalis deal with the three catastrophes of terrorism, starvation, and weak governments. Caught between US sanctions and mismanaged government, Venezuelans flee the hopelessness of their nation's economy. The Holocaust devastated the European Jewish community. In Israel the Nakba eviscerated the Palestinian people. Even the world of rich nations was torn apart by two world wars. Like the prophets, Yeats, a poet from Ireland, cried out in the days between World War I and the War of Irish Independence, "Things fall apart, the center cannot hold; mere anarchy is loosed upon the world, the blood-dimmed tide is loosed."[10] Death ends the political debates; grief and tragedy are the winners.

NO BAD NEWS

Bad news is not well received by regimes whose business is to guarantee that all is well. Governments have their own prophets, religious folk who support the powers that be. The prophets of God, however, do not listen to the prophets of the regimes. Jeremiah wore a yoke to show how Judah and her neighbors needed to submit to the yoke of Babylon or face disaster. The prophet Hananiah, a defender of the government, broke the yoke, saying

---

9. Brueggemann, *Prophetic Imagination*, 45–46.
10. Yeats, "Second Coming," 129.

that things would not be that bad. Jeremiah replied that God was making an iron yoke (Jer 28-29). When Amos said that the king would die and Israel would go into exile, Azariah told him to leave the country and go back to Judah (Amos 7:10-13). Not only was Elijah threatened with death by King Ahab, but friends of the king of Judah also called for the death of Jeremiah and, for a start, put him in a cistern (Jer 38:1-6).

People in power crave legitimacy for their rule, especially if the policies of their government are under threat. Not only does this explain the false prophets defending bad kings, but it also explains why many modern rulers depend on the dominant religion of their nation to support their rule. In Turkey, the president fosters Islam to back his programs. George Bush welcomed the support of evangelicals in invading Iraq. The patriarch of Russian Orthodoxy supports Putin's war in Ukraine. When false prophets, and, in some cases, a whole religious community support unjust and murderous policy, it is dangerous to announce a coming disaster. Prophets have a lonely but necessary mission.

THE OTHER SIDE OF DISASTER

In the face of the military and police power of the state, the prophets lifted up symbols of liberation, of plentiful harvests, and of their divine mission. They were not invented or contrived but were grounded in people's collective memories. Again and again, prophets raised the symbol of the liberation from Egypt. This event, celebrated at the Passover, inscribed the memory of God's deliverance on their hearts. They had been freed from the greatest imperial power of that time (Jer 2:6; Ezek 20:10). Closely related was the symbol of their country as the land of plenty. The first scouts sent into Canaan described a land flowing with milk and honey (Num 13:29). Later, Amos echoed this when he promised a time when the mountains would drip sweet wine (Amos 9:13). Still another symbol was that of the covenant between God and the people. Over and over the prophets reminded the people of the covenant. Jeremiah wrote, "I myself made a covenant with your ancestors when I brought them out of the land of Egypt, out of the house of slavery" (Jer 34:13). Isaiah even used the symbol of the covenant to spell out Israel's mission to the world when he sang, "I am the LORD, I have called you in righteousness, I have taken you by the hand and kept you; I have given you as a covenant to the people, a light to the nations" (Isa 42:6).

Some of these same symbols reappear in the spirituals of Black American slaves dreaming of release. The liberation of slaves from Egypt is at the heart of "Go Down Moses," which ends with the cry, "Let my people go." The song "Deep River" uses the symbol of crossing over Jordan to the promised land as a code for getting slaves across the Ohio River to freedom in the North during the time of the Underground Railroad.[11] Frederick Douglass wrote that for slaves, singing, "Canaan, sweet Canaan, I am bound for the land of Canaan," meant not only heaven but also the North, and "the North was our Canaan."[12]

Not avoiding the coming disaster but looking through it, the prophets opened a skylight with the "poetry of amazement." To a people in despair, captives in a hostile land, the prophet blessed with words of forgiveness, "Comfort, comfort my people, says your God, speak tenderly to Jerusalem . . . Her warfare is ended, that her iniquity is pardoned" (Isa 40:1–2). With this language of amazement, the poet was not changing existing politics but invigorating Israel's imagination. The public recital of God's faithfulness created again Israel's destiny. On the other side of despair is the vision, "How beautiful upon the mountains are the feet of him who brings good tidings . . . who publishes salvation, who says to Zion, 'Your God reigns'" (Isa 52:7).[13]

With a few exceptions the kings of Samaria and Judah failed to practice the radical fairness of the Mosaic provisions for the poor and vulnerable established when God was King. Injustices and immorality grew until there was a historic shift between the city-state system to the imperial system led by Assyria and closely followed by Babylon. That meant the end of Samaria and Jerusalem as independent states. The devastations that followed were unspeakable. The prophetic oracles of doom came true. Do the lamentations of the people of Israel open a window to our future as we face a global system shift?

---

11. Hollie, "Go Down Moshe."
12. Douglas, *My Bondage and My Freedom*, 203.
13. Brueggemann, *Prophetic Imagination*, 67–71.

Chapter 3

Lamentation and Promises

"How lonely sits the city that once was filled with people! How like a widow she has become . . . All her people groan as they search for bread; they trade their treasures for food to revive their strength" (Lam 1:1–2). The book of Lamentations captures the disaster of the fall of Jerusalem to the Babylonians. The warriors had been crushed; the young men and women had gone into captivity. The poet-prophet wept. His eyes flowed with tears. His children were desolate; the enemy prevailed (Lam 1:15–18). Worst of all, it was God who caused the suffering for the multitude of her transgressions (Lam 1:5).

The words of defeat could also be used to describe recent events, such as what happened to Mariupol in Ukraine after its destruction by the Russians. The city was destroyed. Soldiers were killed and captured; some children were taken to Russia to be brought up there. The carnage was displayed on television and in the newspapers. Grandmothers wept; the prisoners wondered where their children were. In another example, Gaza was bombed again; thousands were killed. Children were heard crying for food and water.

The terror unleashed in ancient Judah happened after other devastations and before other events that would be even worse. Jerusalem was destroyed only after the Northern Kingdom of Israel had disappeared into the empire of Assyria. Other towns and cities of Judah had already fallen to the enemy. The future looked even worse. The temple was leveled; the center of their faith was gone. King Zedekiah suffered intolerable grief as he saw his sons executed before his eyes were put out (2 Kgs 25:7). Those who were well off would become captives, carried away across the desert to the enemy's land, never again to see their homes and loved ones.

The future for the residents of Mariupol and Gaza is also bleak. They join the victims of the bombed-out cities of Syria and the agony of Afghanistan. Fleeing drought and conflicts, African migrants cross the sands to drown in the Mediterranean. Guatemalans seek to escape the drug cartels and poverty. Haitians make it to Mexico, attempt to cross the border, and are turned back.

CASCADING FEARS

The increase of refugees and migrants around the world is bold indication that bad things are happening. Those fleeing war make us ask the question whether war will come to us. Nations across the world are increasing their military spending in preparation for conflict. The strongest nations compete to set the rules for the global system. Russia and China seek to recapture lands that they claim, and the West seeks to maintain its wealth and influence. As Russia threatens its nuclear option, North Korea tests intercontinental missiles, and China considers invading Taiwan, we worry about a new world war. According to a Harvard medical report, "War anxiety, sometimes known as nuclear anxiety, is a surprisingly common reaction to the news and images of conflict."[1]

Climate change produces other refugees and migrants. This is troubling for nearly all the nations that are not prepared to deal with these from the poorest nations in the world. Though attempts are made to stop the inflow of immigrants, richer nations are also experiencing destructive weather. Billions of dollars of damage are caused by fires, hurricanes, tornados, and the desertification of ranch lands. Young people are particularly worried. Researchers from the UK's University of Bath and other schools spoke to ten thousand people in ten countries about climate change. Young people between the ages of sixteen and twenty-five said that they were extremely worried.[2]

Lack of good jobs in home countries also creates waves of new immigration. While capitalism promises plenty through trickle-down economics, it does not come soon enough for the millions of young people throughout the world coming onto the job market. In Africa only three

1. Collier, "War Anxiety."
2. Pruitt-Young, "Young People Are Worried."

million jobs are created annually while ten to twelve million youth enter the workforce. This causes more poverty, inequality, crime, and terrorist activities, and leads to even less investment. Africa's youth employment problem has become a global problem with mass migration to richer countries.[3]

The increased numbers of refugees and migrants have raised fears in rich nations. Anti-immigrant sentiment contributed to Brexit in Great Britain, the election of an anti-immigrant candidate in Italy, the growth of right-wing parties in France and Sweden, and calls for a wall on the Mexican border in the United States. The interpenetration of people and their cultures has called into question the concept of ethnically homogenous nations. Since this has much to do with a citizen's identity, reaction against massive immigration is growing and leading to increased polarization their societies.

GLOBAL SYSTEM SHIFTS

Threat of a world war, climate destruction, economic crises, and massive immigration may indicate that a global shift is underway. When Rome fell, it ended the system of the empires of Assyria, Babylon, Persia, Greece, and Rome. Then civilization faltered and human misery increased as warring tribes threatened security and trade. For defense, communities gathered together in enclaves around a castle or fortified city. Instead of widespread trade, communities attempted to be economically self-sufficient. This new system was called feudalism and in Europe lasted nearly a thousand years. That system also came to an end when, in the fifteenth century, capitalism and nation-states emerged. In that system shift, international wars, the slave trade, and the decimation of native populations in the New World took place. If we are facing a new world shift in global systems, we can look forward to more disruption ahead.

From a political and military standpoint, Samaria in the north and Jerusalem in the south did not have a chance. History was making a sharp turn from city-states to empires and these city-states fell. They were not alone. Amos sees the city-states of Damascus, Tyre, Edom, and Gaza being punished (Amos 1:3–12). Jeremiah also includes Egypt, Moab, and even Babylon itself in the coming destruction (Jer 46–51).

Assyria and later Babylon adopted the imperial policy of transporting the elites of Samaria—the rulers, their courts, religious leaders, and

---

3. Donkor, "Africa's Youth Unemployment Crisis."

landowners—back to their lands or other conquered territories. They did the same for other captured cities and moved some of them to the lands of Samaria and Jerusalem. The new mixture of peoples erased the old national identity. The ten tribes of the north disappeared as a recognizable nation. Intermarriage with the newcomers took place and a new people, called Samaritans, came into existence. Ironically, even in the destruction of their nations and national identity, a few of the provisions of land reform emerged as it left the former laborers in the field in some control of the land and of their own destiny.

PROMISES OF GOD'S KINGDOM

Even in horror and terror of Lamentations, God's love and faithfulness is certain. "The steadfast love of the Lord never ceases, his mercies never come to an end" (Lam 3:22). "The Lord will not reject forever. Although he causes grief, he will have compassion" (Lam 3:31). This same refrain is found in all the prophets who told of the destruction and punishment that was to come. These general promises are found in all the prophets. But in many, they are very specific and are related to the blessings that the children of Israel had when God was King.

Faced with a gigantic system shift and deserving of punishment, the leaders and trendsetters of Israel and Judah were taken into captivity. They were refugees again. God's prophets had said it was coming but that was not the end of the story. When God is King—yes, King of refugees—he does not forsake his people but promises to help in some of those same ways. As he had forgiven, fed, provided water, and enabled them to survive and live, he would do it again. They would come back from captivity, and he would again enable them to survive. In the very threat of destruction come the promises and blessings of a time when God would be King again. The promises are not an afterthought. Even before castigating Israel for their abandonment of ethics of the covenant, God promises forgiveness.

Forgiveness

Like a beacon shining through a dark storm-tossed sea comes the promise. "Though your sins are as scarlet, they shall be white as snow; though they are red as crimson, they shall become as wool" (Isa 1:18). What a place for the promise! In Isaiah, it is at the very beginning of a cacophony of crime and punishment. Read today, these words promise forgiveness for police killings, pardon for the pain of the poor, and absolution for those smuggling drugs and migrants.

Not even the unraveling of the nation-state can erase the God's intention for a fresh start. "For I am about to create new heavens and a new earth; the former things shall not be remembered or come to mind" (Isa 65:17). Speaking to Judah, Jeremiah says, "For I will forgive their iniquity, and remember their sin no more" (Jer 31:34). Again, he says, "I will cleanse them from all the guilt of their sin against me, and I will forgive all the guilt of their sin and rebellion against me" (Jer 33:8). After comparing Israel to an unfaithful bride, Hosea wrote of God, "I will heal her disloyalty; I will love them freely, for my anger has turned from them. I will be like the dew to Israel; he shall blossom like the lily" (Hos 14:4–5).

The promised forgiveness is not without cost. It comes at the expense of one who "was wounded for our transgressions, crushed for our iniquities, upon him was the punishment that made us whole, and by his bruises, we are healed" (Isa 53:5).

Plenty to Eat

When massive changes in the world system arrive through war, and now climate change, the prospect of massive hunger looms on the horizon. Poor children in rich nations only get lunch; in parched lands there is almost nothing to eat. Before the destruction of Jerusalem by Nebuchadnezzar "there was no food for the people of the land" (Jer 52:6). In protest the prophets proclaim a new hope. Isaiah writes of those who in the future will live righteously. "They will live on the heights; their refuge will be the fortresses of rocks; their food will be supplied, their water assured. Your eyes will see the king in his beauty" (Isa 33:16–17).

Speaking of the new Jerusalem, Isaiah says, "On this mountain the Lord of hosts will make for all peoples a feast of rich food, a feast of well-matured wines, of rich food filled with marrow" (Isa 25:6). Of this Berrigan writes, "The Grand Feast 'for one and all' reflects the universal theme so dear to Isaiah and the other prophets –Come, everyone, no one outside! God plays the host of the banquet. The Feast is ready, the menu is dwelt upon with pride and anticipation."[4]

---

4. Berrigan, *Isaiah*, 64.

Beyond the captivity of Judah, Jeremiah promises, "They will be radiant over the goodness of the Lord, over the grain, the wine and the oil, and over the young of the flock and their life shall become like a watered garden" (Jer 31:12). Total disbelief must have met these promises when they were first heard amidst the famines of war, drought, and poverty. Yet, these promises plant hope for peace, for migration, or for the next plane bringing relief.

Most important is that the food and drink are promised to last. Even Amos, that devastating critic of Israel, writes of the future, "The time is surely coming says the Lord, when the one who plows shall overtake the one who reaps, and the treader of grapes the one who sows the seed. The mountains will drip sweet wine" (Amos 9:13).

Water in the Wilderness

Few things improve the lives of people more than the availability of pure clean water. With water gardens can be grown, children remain healthy, and women do not have to spend many hours walking just to get water to live.

In the exodus, when God was King, Moses struck a rock and the water poured out. When the Jews were captive in Babylon, the great desert was an obstacle to escape back to Palestine. Even though they were not bound, who could dream about crossing the desert without an easily discovered caravan that could take with it the necessary water? Deliverance would require ample supplies of water in the desert. In the new exodus Isaiah said, "The wilderness and the dry land shall be glad, the desert shall rejoice and blossom, like a crocus it shall bloom abundantly and rejoice with joy and singing" (Isa 35:1-2). Then he added, "The burning sand shall become a pool, and the thirsty ground springs of water" (Isa 35:7). Later, when release from captivity was near, he said, "I will make the wilderness a pool of water and the dry land springs of water" (Isa 41:18). He said again, "I am about to do a new thing; now it springs forth, do you not perceive it? I will make a way in the wilderness and rivers in the desert" (Isa 43:19).

But this was more than a prediction of a way back from captivity; it was the water to bring life in the new exodus from the misery they had experienced. These promises are also good news for people whose suffering includes the actual shortage of water that makes life hard, if not impossible.

As we shall see, these promises have also moved many to provide water to those who need it desperately.

Sick Are Healed

As parents across the world know, one of the best blessings they can have is a healthy child. Our hearts go out to those children who face the challenges of blindness, deafness, or other conditions. While we pray for healing in hospitals in wealthy countries, people in poor nations pray for even more miraculous interventions. Sometimes there are tens of thousands of patients for every doctor and very few hospitals for the whole population. In time of war, earthquakes, floods, and drought, the situation can be even worse.

Among the Jewish people some of the worst illnesses were those that separated people from their communities. The prophets promised that in the coming kingdom the sick would be healed. In Isaiah, God says, "On that day the deaf shall hear the words of a scroll, and out of their gloom and darkness the eyes of the blind shall see" (Isa 29:18). Isaiah writes again, "Then the eyes of the blind shall be opened, and the ears of the deaf unstopped; then the lame shall leap like a deer, and the tongue of the speechless, sing for joy" (Isa 35:5–6).

As important as the promises of physical healing are to those who are obviously in poor health, the prophets also speak to the seemingly healthy. Because God loves his people, God will gather his people and bring forth the blind who have eyes and the deaf who have ears (Isa 43:4–8). Pharisees who tithed their spices but neglected law, justice, mercy, and faith were called blind guides (Matt 23:23–25). Miraculously, one such Pharisee, Nicodemus, did see and heard the good news of the Kingdom (John 3:1–2).

Home and Land

In a world of over 110 million displaced persons,[5] the promise of permanent homes and jobs is sweet indeed. Living on one's own land is not only a pattern for security, but also supplies a deep-seated need within the human heart. Coupled with work that is necessary to support a family, it has become the common dream of all.

---

5. UNHCR, "Refugee Statistics."

By the time of the Assyrian invasion, many common people of Israel and Judah had lost their land to avaricious princes. Then captivity in Babylon erased the hopes and dreams for secure property and the jobs that came from owning good farmland. But to the landless then and now comes the promise, "They shall all sit under their own vines and under their own fig trees, and no one shall make them afraid; for the mouth of the LORD of hosts has spoken" (Mic 4:4). God expressed the same thought in Zechariah. "On that day, says the LORD of hosts, you shall invite each other to come under your vine and fig tree" (Zech 3:10). This brought back to mind the promise of land when God was King.

In the Year of Jubilee, all were to receive back the land free that had been sold in the previous fifty years (Lev 25:13–17). Isaiah refers to this when he says, "The spirit of the Lord is upon me because the Lord has anointed me; he has sent me to bring good news to the oppressed . . . to proclaim the year of the Lord's favor" (Isa 61:1–2). Later Jesus applies this quote to himself and ushers in hope for all the world's people (Luke 4:18–21).

Liberation

In the United States two million people are in prison and make up 22 percent of the entire global prison population. Sixty percent of those are people of color.[6] Families are devastated and a hope for a better future is destroyed. Around the world the dream of liberty lives on for those who are held captive and tortured for their political beliefs and those who are hostages used bargaining chips in global politics.

When God was King, a nation was born of liberated slaves. It was the foundation of the covenant with Israel. God tells Israel, "You have seen what I did to the Egyptians, and how I bore you on eagles' wings and brought you to myself. Now therefore, if you obey my voice and keep my covenant, you shall be my treasured possession out of all the peoples" (Exod 19:4–5). The well-ordered society of Egypt was disrupted by a God of freedom who brought hope for all slaves and prisoners.[7]

The vivid memory of liberation from Egypt became the dream of all the exiles from Judah who lived Babylon. To them Isaiah wrote, "Your sons shall come from far away and your daughters shall be carried on nurse's arms" (Isa 50:4). Then, in jubilee joy, the prophet declares, "He has sent

---

6. Shattuck and Sikkink, "Practice What You Preach," 150–60.

7. Brueggemann, *Prophetic Imagination*, 6–8.

me to bring good news to the oppressed, to bind up the broken-hearted, to proclaim liberty to the captives, and release to the prisoners" (Isa 61:1). With the possibility of release from captivity, the prophet wrote, "Comfort, O comfort my people, says your God. Speak tenderly to Jerusalem and cry to her that she has served her term, that her penalty has been paid" (Isa 40:1).

Swords into Plowshares

It may seem impossible, but the words of Isaiah must come to pass. "He [God] shall judge between the nations, and shall arbitrate for many peoples, they shall beat their swords into plowshares, and their spears into pruning hooks; nation will not lift up sword against nation, neither will they learn war anymore" (Isa 2:4 & Mic 4:3). Berrigan writes, "The words surpass the human even while they engage the human in its deepest longings . . . The words commit, invite, command, exact vows, demand conversion-of hearts as well as swords."[8]

But there is more: "The wolf shall live with the lamb, the leopard shall lie down with the kid, the calf and the lion and the fatling together, and a little child shall lead them" (Isa 11:6). The New World Society will not come through the shedding of blood "but as a recovery of the lost bliss of Eden . . . peace among men, peace in nature, peace with God."[9] Is this just poetry or is it the refugee's almost insane hope that keeps her alive in a refugee camp for years?

Wars happen in the struggle for power within a state as in civil conflict or between states. Yet the whole theme of early biblical history and prophetic literature is the rejection of political power. In the framework of creation, human beings cannot be dominated by fellow humans, but are only led by God.[10] Much more on this subject will be discussed in a later chapter.

---

8. Berrigan, *Isaiah*, 14.
9. Bright, *Kingdom of God*, 92.
10. Mendenhall, *Tenth Generation*, 195.

The Last Kingdom Standing

Victory over Death

Surrounded by the gloom of impending destruction, Isaiah shared the shining vision of a better world of food, water, healing, liberation, home, work, peace, and forgiveness. But we do not live forever in this world. While hope keeps us alive while we are here, our time is limited. If we are saved from wanton destruction, we still get old and die. But Isaiah was not finished. With a poetic leap of faith he wrote, "And he will destroy on this mountain the shroud that is cast over all peoples, the sheet that is spread over all nations; he will swallow up death forever. Then the Lord God will wipe away the tears from all faces" (Isa 25:7–8). No details are given about this victory over death. There is only an all-encompassing hope that will need verification in the future.

While we wait for the ultimate victory over death, the same resurrection hope brings new life to those who despair. Ezekiel is dispatched by God to bring new life to the captives in Babylon, who were virtually dead with despair that they would even again see their homeland. They were pictured as dry bones, dead to hope. God told Ezekiel to prophecy to the wind to blow new life into the bones and behold, they became whole and could breathe again (Ezek 37:1–14).

WHEN GOD WAS KING

When God was King in the desert, there was forgiveness, manna, water, healing, and permanent slavery was but a memory. In Canaan the people were blessed with their own land, homes they did not build, and vineyards they did not plant. With the invasions of Assyria and Babylon all was lost—sovereignty, property, and security. The landed gentry were reduced to slaves and tenant farmers. But the prophets looked beyond the destruction, and the lamentation, to the time when in the lives of the people God again would be King. God would forgive and heal, feed and free, reconcile strangers, and raise the dead; but it was a long time coming.

The imperial system erased all notions of an independent political kingdom like that of David or Solomon. Under the Persian Empire some of the Jews returned to their homeland and struggled to rebuild the temple. The Persians were succeeded by the Greeks under Alexander, who died shortly after his conquests. In the conflict between the followers of Alexander's generals the Jewish community suffered greatly but sought again to establish a kingdom under the Maccabees. After heroic efforts and great courage, there was again a Jewish kingdom. Vertical in structure and possessing coercive power, it was not the Kingdom of God, but an unlovely state to be finally wasted by Rome and Herod.[11]

WILL GOD BE KING AGAIN?

As Jacob lay dying, he blessed his sons, beginning with Reuben, the eldest. When he came to Judah he said, "The scepter shall not depart from Judah" (Gen 49:10). The hired prophet Balaam, still inspired by God, proclaimed, "I see him, but not now; I behold him, but not near; a star shall come out of Jacob, and a scepter shall rise out of Israel" (Num 24:17). In Psalm 2 God declares, "I have set my king on Zion, my holy hill. I will tell of the decree of the Lord. He said to me, 'you are my son; today I have begotten you'" (Ps 2:8–9). There is more to these passages than simply references to David. Another King is coming from Judah, Israel, and God. Isaiah goes into more detail as he sings of the one who is to come.

> For a child has been born for us, a son given to us; authority rests upon his shoulders; and he is named Wonderful Counselor, Mighty God, Everlasting Father, Prince of Peace. His authority shall grow continually, and there shall be endless peace for the throne of David and his kingdom. He will establish and uphold it with justice and with righteousness from this time onward and forevermore. (Isa 9:6–7)

Upholding peace with justice is key is the task of the coming King. Rightfully so, because with justice the blessings of the Kingdom come. With justice there is endless peace, liberation, and land. With justice there is also food, water, and a chance for healing. To the ancient ear and modern realism, justice implies a coercive regime that enforces laws that assure fairness and human rights. But in a direct line with the history of Israel before the monarchy, Isaiah speaks of a figure who will bring justice in another way. In that day only a king could bring justice, but Isaiah describes a totally different kind of king. He will bring justice to the nations, not just to Israel. He will not have a noisy campaign because he will not lift up his voice. Gentle, he will not break a bruised reed or snuff out a flickering wick. With

---

11. Bright, *Kingdom of God*, 178–85.

unbelievable endurance he will not be faint or crushed until he has brought justice to the world (Isa 42:14).

How is this possible? God already named him before he was born. His weapons will be words because God made his mouth a two-edged sword. His mission will be for far more than Israel. He will be a light to the nations (Isa 49:1–8). The words he speaks will not only cut through lies and deceit, but God will also give him the tongue of a teacher to sustain the weary with a word (Isa 50:4). Unlike the good looks of Saul and David, this king has no form of majesty that we should look at him, nothing in his appearance that we should desire him. Yes, the justice of a king could help provide the blessings of food, shelter, water, healing, and liberation. But what about forgiveness and death? Isaiah continued, "He was wounded for our transgressions and crushed for our iniquities . . . For he was cut off from the lands of the living, stricken for the transgression of my people" (Isa 53:2–8).

At the time of imperial rule of Babylon and Persia, the political implications of this vision of kingship made it a nonstarter. In the current struggle of world leadership between the United States and Europe on one hand confronted by Russia and China on the other side, this Kingdom also does not make any sense. Yet, as we shall see, it may be the only way out. It may well be *The Last Kingdom Standing*.

Chapter 4

The Kingdom of God Is Near

THE FIRST RECORDED WORDS of Jesus are, "The time is fulfilled, the kingdom of God is near, repent and believe in the good news" (Mark 1:15). Reference to that announcement is repeated often in the Gospels and becomes the message of the disciples (Luke 9:2). Though it is the chief proclamation of Jesus in the Gospels, people continue to debate its meaning. What is the "Kingdom of God?"

IS IT ABOUT HEAVEN?

In the middle of the nineteenth century theologian Friedrich Schleiermacher located the Kingdom of God within the individual stimulated by a Christ-consciousness. He was followed by Albrecht Ritschl, who believed that after being redeemed by Christ believers should work to establish the Kingdom of God in this world.[1] In the twentieth century Walter Rauschenbush continued this emphasis on the Kingdom of God. For him, the Kingdom of God was a revolutionary movement that Christ initiated and sustains. Christ is the power behind it and fashions its force.[2] For his position on the Kingdom of God Rauschenbusch was considered a major proponent of the "social gospel."

Based on his reading of the Gospels, Johannes Weiss believed that the Kingdom of God did not come at the time of Jesus, but its actualization was yet to come. The Kingdom was about the last things, called "eschatology." It

---

1. Perrin, *Kingdom of God*, 14–15.
2. Rauschenbusch, *Righteousness of the Kingdom*, 112.

The Last Kingdom Standing

was not the task of people but was solely the work of God. Only Jesus can battle again the devil and gather his disciples to wait for the Kingdom of God.[3] In his work Weiss does little with the Old Testament promises but concentrates on the Jewish apocalyptic vision of the struggle between God and Satan. This is found in Jewish literature written at the time of the New Testament, as in the *Assumption of Moses*.[4] Weiss's reference to the battle between God and Satan in Jewish apocalyptic writings does do much to explain the many references to Jesus casting out demons.

Following Weiss, Albert Schweitzer also challenged the view that Jesus was initiating the Kingdom of God in his lifetime and that it was the task of his followers to work toward its fulfillment. For Schweitzer, the idea that Jesus founded the Kingdom of God on earth and preached an ethic of the Kingdom was just a message designed by rationalism, endowed with life by liberalism, and clothed in historical garb by modern theology.[5] For Weiss and Schweitzer, the realization of the Kingdom of God will only come in the next world. This view of the Kingdom of God influenced a number of theologians like Barth, Bultmann, Conzelmann, Bornkamm, and others.[6]

This view, that the Kingdom of God is really about heaven and the church's message of salvation, is also the understanding of many Christians across the world. In Matthew, the Kingdom is called the "Kingdom of Heaven" instead of the "Kingdom of God" as is found in the other Gospels. This is because in writing to a Jewish audience, Matthew did not want to use God's name needlessly. However, this language causes many casual readers of Matthew to interpret the Kingdom of God as heaven and the path to salvation—a view supported by many common sermons.

IS IT ABOUT THE HERE AND NOW?

While most modern theologians accept that the Kingdom of God is about the last things and heaven, many have said that God's Kingdom is also coming to the earth now. Breaking with the consistent eschatology of Weiss and Schweitzer, C. H. Dodd used the phrase "realized eschatology." He viewed the Kingdom of God as being both a future fulfillment and its beginning

---

3. Weiss, *Jesus' Proclamation of the Kingdom of God*, 129–130.
4. Tromp, *Assumption of Moses*, 19.
5. Schweitzer, *Quest for the Historical Jesus*, 219.
6. Bultmann, "Introduction," in Weiss, *Jesus' Proclamation of the Kingdom*, 26–27.

here and now.[7] Dodd based much of his position on Jesus' parables of the Kingdom. He was joined in this view by Jeremias. He also made the point that the message of Jesus was that the Kingdom was both in the present and in the future.[8]

Jürgen Moltmann also opened the door to the Kingdom of God breaking in on our world when he appealed to a Hebrew instead of a Greek way of thinking. While the Greeks thought in "static" categories, the Hebrews thought of "promise" and unfolding. Moltmann pointed out that identifying the Kingdom of God with eschatology was a static concept very foreign to the Bible. Rather, dwelling on the promises of the Kingdom, one might naturally think of promises coming to fulfillment. Though partial now, the God of present and future will bring them to pass.[9] Far more has been written on this issue, but for this study we will simply welcome Jesus' announcement of the Kingdom as referring both to the eternal future and also to the here and now.

THE REIGN OF GOD?

Is the Kingdom the "Reign of God"? Some seeking to modernize the concept of the "Kingdom" have called it the "Reign of God." This is certainly in line with the concept of the Kingdom in the Jewish apocalyptic literature written near the time of Christ. In the *Assumption of Moses*, speaking of the Kingdom, the writer said that the heavenly one will rise from his royal throne and go out from his holy habitation with anger and wrath, and the earth will tremble.[10] Tracing the origins of the Kingdom, Perrin described God's sovereignty over the nations.[11] Numerous other books have been published about the Kingdom with the "Reign of God" in the title or subtitle, like Mortimer Arias's *Announcing the Reign of God*.[12]

While the Kingdom involves God's reign and power, that is not its chief message. Back when God was King, he first bestowed his bountiful gifts. His punishing power was only seen when those gifts were rejected, scorned, or forgotten. Even the laws given and observed to this day were

---

7. Dodd, *Parables of Jesus*, 33.
8. Perrin, *Kingdom of God*, 81.
9. Moltmann, *Theology of Hope*, 40–42.
10. Tromp, *Assumption of Moses*, 19.
11. Perrin, *Kingdom of God*, 44.
12. Arias, *Announcing the Reign of God*.

only issued after the liberation from Egypt and their mutual partnership in the covenant. Contrary to the late Jewish wish for God's destruction of Israel's enemies under God's reign, Jesus meant something else when he announced the Kingdom.

GOOD NEWS OF THE KINGDOM

What is the Kingdom of God? We learn most about the Kingdom when Jesus says, "believe the good news" (Mark 1:15). In some translations of the Bible the Greek word for "good news" is translated as "the gospel." Modern readers are quick to relate that to Paul's message that through the sacrifice of Christ on the cross and his resurrection we receive the forgiveness of sins and the hope of heaven. That certainly is included in the good news of the Kingdom but it is only one of the many blessings included in coming of the Kingdom. At the time of Jesus's announcement of the Kingdom, he had not yet suffered and died. His resurrection was a future event. What was the good news for Jesus' first listeners? What is the Kingdom of God for us today?

If the Kingdom is not the "reign" of God, it is the "blessings" of God. The coming of the Kingdom is the repetition of the blessings to Israel when God was King. It is also the fulfillment of the promises of the prophets. No doubt, many in Israel hoped for God to come and destroy Israel's enemies, yet others remembered the time when God was King and the promises of God in the prophets. The good news of the Kingdom was really about forgiveness, food, water, healing, jobs and homes, liberation, peace between nations, and the end of death. Of course, good news of this kind was met with skepticism. It seemed impossible then and is just as unbelievable now.

JESUS' WORLD AND OURS

In the dark and despairing days of Roman Judea there was no justice. An occupying power taxed the people illegally to support their troops. Politically the nation was polarized between collaborators and terrorists. Religion was about debating minutiae, while staying clear of law, justice, and mercy. Knowing that Jerusalem was ripe for destruction, Jesus wept (Luke 19:41).

Under a foreign "authoritarian" government, with radical prejudice against foreigners, self-righteous fundamentalists, and religious patriots, Jesus announced that the Kingdom of God was at hand (Mark 1:15). It was the alternative to everything they knew. The concept was not new but now there was an immediacy to it. In that context it was subversive. But it was also awe-inspiring. If God was King and that kingship involved this world, everything could be different.

Today, climate change, pandemics, coming conflict, and refugees are world crises. The stakes are unimaginably grim. No nation can adequately deal with them. When these crises are coupled with the already unequal divisions of wealth, access to healthcare, housing, and widespread unemployment of young people, the stage is set for disaster. Climate conferences come up short. The World Health Organization cannot provide vaccines for poor nations. The UN cannot stop the coming conflict between the US and China and even now, before it gets worse, refugees, political and economic, are everywhere waiting.

JESUS' MIRACLES AND MESSAGE

The pattern was clear. When God was King, when there was an emergency, dramatic miracles broke into people's depression and despair. The waters parted, manna appeared, waters came from the rock, sins were forgiven as snake bites healed, farms were gifts, and victory was won. Then came the message: as you have been liberated, you should free others. With a sin offering forgiveness was always available. God would reward faithfulness with good rainfall. There were regulations for good health and regular land reform. Obedience to these provisions would also be rewarded with victory in battle for peace.

The Kingdom of God Is the Forgiveness of Sins

While skeptics stood nearby, Jesus miraculously healed a man of palsy and forgave his sin. Only God can forgive sins, the skeptics said. Jesus replied that the Son of Man has power on earth the forgive sins (Luke 5:17–24). He widened that message when he told his disciples, "If you forgive the sins of any, they are forgiven them; if you retain the sins of any, they are retained" (John 20:23). Then came the warning, "if you do not forgive others, neither will your father forgive your trespasses" (Matt 6:15).

The Kingdom of God Is Feeding the Hungry and Giving Water to the Thirsty

Emergencies happen. Miraculously, five thousand were fed (Mark 6:37–44), and later four thousand (Mark 8:4–9). The promise of God also included wine as Isaiah wrote, "On this mountain the LORD of hosts will make for all peoples a feast of rich food, a feast of well-aged wines, of rich food filled with marrow, of well-aged wines strained clear" (Isa 25:6). In another emergency Jesus turned water into the best wine and Jesus' disciples believed in him (John 2:1–11). Jesus' message was in the Kingdom prayer, "give us this day our daily bread" (Matt 6:11). Jesus also taught that in the future we should feed the hungry when he said, "For I was hungry, and you gave me food, I was thirsty, and you gave me something to drink" (Matt 25:35).

On a deeper level, in the Gospel of John Jesus addresses both those who have no bread and those who have enough bread but have a deeper hunger. He says, "I am the bread of life. Whoever comes to me will never be hungry, and whoever believes in me will never be thirsty" (John 6:35). What was true of bread is also true of water. Jesus tells the woman at the well, "Everyone who drinks of this water will be thirsty again, but for those who drink of the water that I will give them will never be thirsty. The water I will give them will become in them a spring of water gushing up to eternal life" (John 4:13–14).

The Kingdom of God Is Healing the Sick.

When God was King, Miriam was healed from her leprosy. In Jesus' time, Jesus healed first one leper (Matt 8:2–3) and then ten more (Luke 17:12–14). The prophets told of a time when the lame would leap. Then Jesus told a lame man to get up and walk (John 5:8). Isaiah said that the blind would see and the deaf would be healed (Isa 35:5), and then Jesus gave sight to the blind (Mark 8:2–4; 10:51). He healed the man who was deaf and dumb who then could hear and speak (Mark 7:32–36). The power to do these miracles was even passed on to Jesus' disciples. In sending them out he said, "As you go, proclaim the good news, 'The kingdom of heaven has come near.' Cure the sick, raise the dead, cleanse the lepers, cast out demons" (Matt 10:7–8). The message for those of us who cannot do the miracles of the first disciples is to do what we can. Jesus said, "I was sick, and you took care of me" (Matt 25:36).

The Kingdom of God Is Economic Fairness

Although it was too late for the land reform of the Jubilee, Jesus stressed economic fairness in an unequal world. On this topic, there is not much in the way of miracles unless we count Jesus seeing Zacchaeus in a Sycamore tree. Jesus' encounter with Zaccheus moved the rich tax collector to share his wealth (Luke 19:5). Jesus' message was unequivocal. At Nazareth he defined his ministry in the words of Isaiah, "He has anointed me to bring good news to the poor . . . to proclaim the year of the Lord's favor" (Luke 4:18–19). For Isaiah and Jesus, the Jubilee in Leviticus 25 was the year of the Lord's favor. The rich do not do well. Jesus told the story of a rich man in Hades in torment while the poor man, Lazarus, is in Abraham's bosom (Luke 16:19–35). At another time Jesus said, "It is easier for a camel to go through the eye of a needle than for someone who is rich to enter the kingdom of God" (Matt 19:24). That makes sense. If the Kingdom is economic fairness, someone who is rich at the expense of the poor has no place in the Kingdom.

On a more profound level Jesus says that the Kingdom is like laborers in the vineyard. Those who worked the whole day received their wages. Those who only worked a few hours received the same wages. In this case the last (those without work) will be first and those hired first would be last because of the owner's generosity (Matt 20:1–13). Had the Jubilee been observed over the years, they would all have had their own land. This is Jesus' way of fulfilling the prophecy that all would enjoy their own vine and fig tree, their own home and job.

The Kingdom of God Is Liberation

When God was King, he liberated the people of Israel from Egypt. When the Jews were under Cyrus, God aroused him to set the exiles free (Isa 45:13). Jesus quoted Isaiah: "He has sent me to proclaim release to the captives" (Luke 4:18). Later the apostles who had been in prison were freed when an angel of the Lord opened the prison doors (Acts 5:17–20). Though we are not able to open prison doors, Jesus' message to us is, "I was in prison, and you visited me" (Matt 25:36).

Liberation was more than freeing prisoners. Jesus liberated a man from an unclean spirit (Mark 1:23–26) and set free another from a legion of demons (Mark 5:1–19). He also told the story of how a slave who invested wisely was given charge over ten cities (John 8:34–36). Not all slavery is physical. Jesus said, "Truly I tell you, everyone who commits sin is a slave to sin . . . so if the Son sets you free, you will be free indeed" (John 8:34–36).

The Kingdom of God Is Peace between Nations

Micah wrote, "He shall judge between many peoples, and shall arbitrate between strong nations far away; they shall beat their swords into plowshares, and their spears into pruning hooks; nation shall not lift up sword against nation, neither shall they learn war anymore" (Mic 4:3). As with the other promises, this never came to pass in Jesus' ministry, or since. But the mustard seed was planted when Jesus healed the slave of the enemy centurion (Matt 8:5–11). He also commended the Syrophoenician woman's faith in her request to cast the demon out of her daughter (Mark 7:26).

Clearly Jesus was different from Judah Maccabeus. Judah, or "the Hammer," as he was known, waged a three-year guerilla war against Antiochus of Syria two hundred years before Jesus. He cleansed the temple and protected Israel by the sword. After the time of Jesus there was another messianic figure, Simon Bar-Giora, whose goal was to defeat the Romans, cleanse the temple, and establish his own kingdom. His rule also depended upon sword and spear. His efforts ended with the fall of Jerusalem and destruction of the temple.[13] Tried by Pilate as "King of the Jews," Jesus redefined kingship. His Kingdom was not "from" this world; otherwise, his servants would fight (John 18:36). It was, and is, a Kingdom. But it is one of soft power instead of one of coercion enforced by sword and spear. There will be more on this in chapter 9.

The Kingdom of God Defeats Death

Isaiah had written, "He will destroy on this mountain the shroud that is cast over all peoples, the sheet that is spread over all nations: he will swallow up death forever" (Isa 25:7). Jesus' miracles opened the doors to the reality of the resurrection. He raised the daughter of Jairus (Luke 8:54–56). He also raised his friend Lazarus (John 11:41–44). Of course, their resurrections were not permanent. One day they would die again. As he prayed at Lazarus's tomb, Jesus asked that it be a sign that he had been sent by God and

---

13. Wright, *Simply Jesus*, 106–7, 114–16.

that his words might be believed. His teaching continues for all: "I am the resurrection and the life, those who believe in me, though they die, will live, and everyone who lives and believes in me will never die" (John 11:25–26).

Even more important in the story of the Kingdom is that Christ is the Messiah spoken of in Isaiah, where so many promises of the Kingdom are found. He was wounded for our transgressions, crushed for our iniquities; upon him was the punishment that made us whole (Isa 53:5). After his resurrection he again explained to his disciples and us, "Thus it is written that the Messiah is to suffer and rise from the dead on the third day, that repentance and forgiveness of sins is to be proclaimed to all nations" (Luke 24:46–47). As Isaiah said, "He will swallow death forever" (Isa 25:8).

PARABLES OF THE KINGDOM

But where is food for the hungry, water for drought, and healing in a cancer ward? Where is a home and job for those living in the slums of Mumbai or the Kakuma refugee camp in Kenya? Will there ever be liberation for the thousands of political prisoners around the world? Will peace come to Ukraine and Gaza? Will there be forgiveness for war crimes and massive theft? For many, the promises of the Kingdom simply have not come to pass. Faced with the idea that fulfillment of the Kingdom promises would happen all at once, Johannes Weiss simply concluded that Jesus was mistaken.[14]

It was from studying the parables that C. H. Dodd, and many who followed him, came to believe in a realized eschatology, which held that Jesus was speaking about a Kingdom of the future that was also partially being realized in the present.[15] Promises for food, forgiveness, healing, and the other blessings would never be fully realized in this world. The Kingdom was not a slam dunk. Instead, it was like a field where good seeds were planted but an enemy planted weeds (Matt 13:24–30, 36–43). It was like a fish net thrown into the sea that caught both good and bad fish (Matt 13:47–50). From the time of Jesus, it is like a mustard seed, with just a small beginning, but it will grow in the future to provide shelter for many (Matt 13:31–32), or like just a little yeast that will leaven the whole dough (Matt 13:33). These parables are especially valuable for those who are easily depressed because their hopes are dashed for peace, liberation, the end of

---

14. Weiss, *Jesus; Proclamation of the Kingdom*, 84–89.

15. Dodd, *Parables of the Kingdom*. See also Jeremias, *Rediscovering the Parables*; Bright, *Kingdom of God*; and Wright, *Simply Jesus* and *When God Was King*.

hunger, full employment, and other blessings of the Kingdom. Even so, the knowledge that there will be the inevitable growth of a seed and of leaven is enough to find a glorious purpose in life. It is like finding a treasure in a field and selling all to buy the field or finding a pearl of great price (Matt 13:44–45).

What is the strategy for the realization of the Kingdom of God? It comes from the word of the Kingdom. It is about forgiveness and the hope of heaven, but it is also about healing and employment, liberation, and peace. It is a sower who spread seeds over the ground. The results are spotty, as not all seeds take root. Jesus prepared his disciples for disappointment. But by including the seeds that grew and multiplied in his parable, Jesus prepared his disciples for joy (Matt 13:1–9, 18–23).

REPENT AND BELIEVE THE GOOD NEWS

With reference to the Kingdom of God, what did Jesus mean when he said, "repent"? Traditionally, believers might examine themselves by going through the Ten Commandments. While certainly a laudable practice, how does this prepare us for the cornucopia of the good news of the Kingdom? Jesus is much more specific in his ethics of the Kingdom in Matthew 25:

> I was hungry, and you gave me food, I was thirsty, and you gave me something to drink, I was a stranger and you welcomed me, I was naked, and you gave me clothing, I was sick and you took care of me, I was in prison and you visited me.' Then the righteous will answer him, 'Lord, when was it that we saw you hungry and gave you food, or thirsty and gave you something to drink? And when was it that we saw you a stranger and welcomed you, or naked and gave you clothing? And when was it that we saw you sick or in prison and visited you?' And the king will answer them, 'Truly I tell you, just as you did it to one of the least of these who are members of my family, you did it to me." (Matt 25:35–40)

One of the criticisms of the liberal interpretation of the Kingdom of God by theologians like Ritschl is that they put the emphasis upon the activity of men for building the Kingdom of God. The emphasis in the Gospels is that the Kingdom comes because of the activity of God as King.[16] As Jesus forgave, healed, fed, and taught, it was evident that through him God was King and brought about the blessings of the Kingdom. But as Jesus sent

---

16. Perrin, *Kingdom of God*, 7.

out his disciples then and now, his followers have the privilege and duty to share these blessings of the Kingdom to those who need them most.

Repentance then is a fitting command for us to examine ourselves to see how well we have been part of God's mission to bring about the blessings of the Kingdom. This is certainly true when opportunities present themselves in our personal lives. But is it not also true of our participation in our work, our communities, and our government? To repent means to reexamine our ideologies, our loyalties, and our selfishness to see how we might better work with God building the Kingdom.

As difficult as it is to repent, it may be even more difficult to believe the good news of the coming of the Kingdom. When Jesus' Jewish hearers first heard that message, they thought about the promises of the Kingdom. It was difficult then, and is difficult now, to believe that the Kingdom of God, with its cornucopia of good things, could be realized in the context of a sinful world. For people who have lived many years, for others who know history, for still others who counsel the troubled, it is easy to become skeptical. Skepticism even flows from some teachings of the Christian faith. One such teaching is the doctrine of original sin, which declares that all people are selfish, self-seeking, and by nature will care more for themselves than others. Another teaching is that of the last days when we are to expect great tribulation with wars and rumors of wars (Matt 24:6–8). Still another teaching is that the poor we will have with us always (Matt 26:11). This is commonly believed to mean that poverty for some is a preordained reality.

The problem with skepticism is that while it has its roots both in life experiences and also in some Christian teachings, it has a way of coloring people's observations, even when no skepticism is called for. For example, it might be pointed out that many people have been aided in helping themselves get out of poverty. Rather than greeting that fact with joy, a skeptic might think, "Well, that is just an isolated example" or "That probably will not work elsewhere."

Once a person looks at life through a skeptic's eyes, the challenges of the Kingdom can be simply dismissed. There will never be total peace, so why work for it? Rich people will always fight against the redistribution of resources, so why work for something as idealistic or foolish as that? As is readily apparent, skepticism is a way of protecting ourselves from both repentance and also the possibility of bringing about the good things of the Kingdom.

The biblical perspective, however, suggests that the gospel of salvation is more powerful than the ugly reality of original and actual sin. Paul said, "But where sin increased, grace abounded all the more" (Rom 5:20). In terms of personal forgiveness, most Christians believe that no matter how terrible our sin, Christ's suffering, death, and resurrection more than atone for it. Thus, the gospel is more powerful than sin. This does not contradict the terrible reality of sin and human greed. It simply states that Christ has conquered sin and death. If this is true with regard to personal sin and guilt, is it also true with the Kingdom of God, the New World Society? Can people really believe that the good things of the Kingdom can come in life as we know it? The answer both from Scriptures and history is a resounding *yes*! However, it will not come from the outside with someone else providing it for us. It only comes through the work of God with the personal involvement of people changing their lifestyles and believing the good news.

The gospel is good news except for people who take great comfort in only believing bad news. Therefore, the gospel of the Kingdom requires a conversion from being a skeptic to being a believer who works in the Kingdom. Believing the gospel means that every day is greeted with Christ's own optimism when he said, "My father is working still, and I am working" (John 5:17). When people really believe that the promises of the Kingdom are coming to pass, this shows that they have been born from above (John 3:3). For unless one has had this experience of having one's vision changed, one cannot see the Kingdom of God.

Chapter 5

The Kingdom in Cross and Conflict

THE KINGDOM OF GOD is coming, like the grain ripening in the field or the growth of the mustard seed. At the same time the resistance to the Kingdom is described in Matthew 25 when Jesus calls out those who would not feed the hungry, give water to the thirsty, welcome migrants, or visit the sick and prisoners. Like two tectonic plates in seismic tension prior to an earthquake, something must give.

THE KINGDOM COMES

The Kingdom that Jesus announced soon got noticed. Thousands of people followed him and wanted to hear and see more (Mark 14:14–21). Like many others at the time, John the Baptizer was looking for an apocalyptic political victory. That was not to come, but the Kingdom was still quite visible. Jesus said, "Go and tell John what you hear and see: the blind receive their sight, the lame walk, the lepers are cleansed, the deaf hear, the dead are raised, and the poor have good news brought to them" (Matt 11:4–5).

Jesus' words of judgement also caused consternation. He said, "it is easier for a camel to go through the eye of a needle than for someone who is rich to enter the kingdom of God" (Matt 19:24). He warned the Pharisees, "Woe to you, scribes and Pharisees, hypocrites! For you clean the outside of the cup and of the plate, but inside they are full of greed and self-indulgence" (Matt 23:25). As the Maccabees once cleansed the sanctuary of the temple because of the defilement by the Greeks (1 Macc 4:36–59), now Jesus cleansed the temple governed by the high priest as a "den of robbers" (Matt 21:13).

The Last Kingdom Standing

THE RESISTANCE GROWS

Grinding against the coming Kingdom of blessings and judgment was the tectonic plate of institutionalized evil. Applied to the monarchy after Solomon, Brueggemann called it "royal consciousness."[1] Applied in Jesus' time, it meant accepting the accommodation to Roman rule by the leadership of Israel. As much as crowds of people welcomed Jesus as the Messiah, the establishment did not. Though they differed theologically, the Pharisees and Sadducees came together to confront Jesus. The Pharisees and Sadducees came to Jesus and asked him to show them a sign from heaven (Matt 16:1). Later the Pharisees and Herodians asked him about taxes, hoping either to get him arrested as a tax evader or have him lose his popularity with the nationalists (Matt 22:16–21). Again, the chief priests, the scribes, and the elders asked him by what authority Jesus was doing these things (Mark 11:28). Here was the real issue. Jesus was attacking the established powers simply by accomplishing what they were unable to do. This was a criticism that they could not tolerate.

Two days before the Passover, the chief priests and scribes are looking for a way to secretly arrest and kill Jesus. In the rising tension Judas volunteers to betray Jesus to them. In the darkness, where shadows obscure features, Judas shows the soldiers whom to arrest by giving Jesus a kiss. Jesus is then taken to the assembled high priest, the chief priests, the scribes, and the elders. There was no higher court within the government of Israel. However, as an occupied power, they could not execute him. As soon as it was morning they took him to Pilate, the Roman procurator of Judea (Mark 14:42—15:5).

THE CROSS

The crucifixion of Christ did not simply happen. Jesus knew it would happen. As he proclaimed the Kingdom, he also proclaimed his death and resurrection. This was not to be a disheartening surprise event. Jesus would undergo great suffering, be rejected by Israel's elite, and be killed. Then three days later he would rise from the dead. Taking him aside, Peter rebuked him, but Jesus pressed on. "If any want to become my followers, let them deny themselves and take up their cross and follow me" (Mark 8:34).

---

1. Brueggemann, *Prophetic Imagination*, 21–37.

The Kingdom in Cross and Conflict

As if that was not enough, Jesus repeated the warning a little time later, "The Son of Man is betrayed into human hands, and they will kill him, and three days after being killed, he will rise again," but they did not understand what he was saying but were afraid to ask him (Mark 11:31–32). Then a third time, as Jesus and his followers were going up to Jerusalem amidst rising tensions, Jesus said, "See, we are going up to Jerusalem, and the Son of Man will be handed over to the chief priests and scribes, and they will condemn him to death, then they will hand him over to the Gentiles; they will mock him, and spit upon him, and flog him, and kill him, and after three days he will rise again" (Mark 10:33–34).

N. T. Wright asked, "How can the suffering and death of Israel's Messiah somehow bring about his worldwide sovereign kingdom? Or conversely what can the establishment of God's sovereign rule on earth as in heaven have to do with the brutal execution of Jesus?"[2] He went on to draw a contrast between the theologies of the reformers, who saw in the crucifixion the atonement of sinners, and the theologies of those with an emphasis on God's liberation of the oppressed and "options for the poor." Wright believes that those stressing the forgiveness of sins need to examine the Gospels more closely to better understand the significance of the crucifixion for the Kingdom. On the other hand, he wants those emphasizing aid for the poor to come to grips with the meaning of the crucifixion.[3]

Was Jesus' death and resurrection the culmination of a Kingdom event or was it chiefly the sacrifice for sins and victory over death? Much depends upon the definition of the Kingdom. Is the Kingdom, as stated by Wright, "the establishment of God's worldwide sovereign Kingdom"? If so, the forgiveness of sins is an "add-on" contributed by Paul and much of the rest of the New Testament. However, if the Kingdom of God is not the sovereign rule but rather the gifts of God, then the forgiveness of sins and our resurrection is the very heartbeat of the Kingdom.

The promises of the prophets for food, water, healing, liberation, land, and peace are all dependent upon forgiveness. The vicious sins of pre-exilic Israel were the cause of the destruction of Israel and Judah. For the promises to be fulfilled, sins needed to be revealed, confessed, and forgiven. Is this true of global warming, swarms of refugees, failed states, and a new global war? Those preaching the cross for the forgiveness of sins may need to probe more deeply what sins have contributed to the world problems we

2. Wright, *How God Became King*, 176.
3. Wright, *How God Became King*, 176–78.

face, how the cross forgives, and how the resurrection enables God to build the Kingdom among us.

CONFLICT

Before Jesus died, he wept over Jerusalem. He had wept before when Lazarus died (John 11:35). Then it was over a friend, now it was over a city, a nation, a culture, and the temple, the meeting place of God and humanity (Luke 19:41). The seismic tension between the tectonic plates of the coming of the Kingdom and the world's sin had been clearly revealed in Jesus' crucifixion. Now the resulting earthquake would cause the destruction of Jerusalem. He said, "The days will come upon you when your enemies will set up ramparts around you and surround you and hem you in on every side. They will crush you to the ground, you and your children within you and they will leave not one stone upon another; because you did not know the time of your visitation from God" (Luke 19:43-44). Escape might be necessary. When Jerusalem is surrounded, you can know that destruction has come near. Go to the mountains, leave the city. Woe to those who are pregnant and nursing. Captives will be taken, and Jerusalem will be trampled (Luke 21:20-24).

The earthquake continues. You will hear of wars and insurrections; nation will rise up against nation and in various places there will be plagues and famines. Jesus' Kingdom workers will not escape. They will be arrested and persecuted, handed over to synagogues to be tried and prisons to be punished. They will testify before kings and governors because of Jesus' name. They will be betrayed by their own families, and some will be put to death. They will be hated by all because of Jesus' name. But with all this happening—yes, it is unbelievable—"Not a hair on your head will perish" (Luke:2:9-18). How can someone be killed yet not have a hair on their head perish? This is the teaching that, inevitably, the Kingdom comes in conflict. Yet, Jesus' followers will survive in this life or the next.

BLESSINGS OF THE KINGDOM

Like bookends, the Kingdom of God is at the beginning and the end of Acts. At the beginning of Acts the disciples ask, "Lord, is this the time when you will restore the Kingdom to Israel?" (Acts 1:6). Then, concluding in the last verses, Luke writes, "He [Paul] lived there two whole years at his own expense and welcomed all who came to him, proclaiming the kingdom of God and teaching about the Lord Jesus Christ with all boldness and without hindrance." (Acts 28:30–31). The Kingdom in Acts is not just for Israel; it is for all people. With the Spirit disciples would be witnesses to the ends of the earth (Acts 1:8).

The Forgiveness of Sins

In reaction to Peter's powerful sermon on Pentecost, the people were cut to the heart and said to Peter and the other disciples, "'Brothers, what shall we do?' Peter said to them, 'Repent and be baptized, every one of you in the name of Jesus Christ so that your sins might be forgiven'" (Acts 2:38). After escaping from prison, Peter again went to the temple. There he was taken to the high priest. Explaining that they must obey God rather than men, Peter said of Jesus that God had exalted him as Leader and Savior that he might give repentance to Israel and forgiveness of sins (Acts 5:27–31). Called by Cornelius, Peter also brought him the good news. He said, "All the prophets testify about him that everyone who believes in him receives forgiveness of sins through his name" (Acts 10:43).

Paul continued speaking of forgiveness. Preaching to a Jewish audience in the synagogue in Antioch, Pisidia, he said of Jesus, "Let it be known to you therefore, my brothers, that through this man forgiveness of sins is proclaimed to you" (Acts 13:38). Later in front of King Agrippa Paul tells the story of his life as a persecutor of Christians and then of his conversion on the road to Damascus. Then he reveals the whole purpose of his mission: "to open their eyes so that they may turn from darkness to light and from the power of Satan to God, so that they may receive forgiveness of sins" (Acts 26:18). While forgiveness was key to the Kingdom blessings, it was only one of the others bestowed in the mission of the early church.

Sharing Land and Property

With the coming of the Spirit at Pentecost, thousands came to faith and were baptized. With such events of joy, dimmed a bit by the antagonism of the authorities, believers set about to relive the Jubilee with respect to property (Lev 25). "All who believed were together and had all things in common. They would sell their possessions and goods and distribute the proceeds to all, as any had need" (Acts 2:43–45). This was not just an afterthought but was the direct result of the apostle's proclamation. "With great power the apostles gave their testimony to the resurrection of the Lord Jesus and great grace was upon them all. There was not a needy person among them, for as many as owned land or houses sold them and brought the proceeds of what was sold" (Acts 4:33–34). Apparently, no one bothered with the legal questions concerning the property. The things of this age had become inconsequential.[4]

Since that time sacrificial giving for the sake of the needy has always been a part of Christian practice. It has also become a model for those with great properties and large resources to help those with nothing. Although here, the story of Ananias and Sapphira is most instructive. Having misrepresented their gifts by claiming to give more than they gave, they both died (Acts 5:1–11). That may well be a warning to those who wish to make a name for themselves with great generosity while keeping back for themselves far more than they need for a comfortable life.

Taking care to the poor and needy did not end with the biblical accounts. The Christian philosopher Aristides wrote the following to Emperor Hadrian around 125 AD: "They despise not the widow, and grieve not the orphan. He that hath distributeth liberally to him that hath not."[5] As was the case with the crises in Jerusalem after the resurrection, Christian continued to respond to emergencies in the succeeding years. After barbarians laid waste to Numidia in northern Africa and left many Christians homeless, Cyprian collected contributions of one hundred thousand sesterces for those who had been affected.[6] Indeed, Christians have been at the forefront of aid for the vulnerable throughout the ages. Should conflicts abound and disaster spread in another global system shift, God will again bring aid, and Christians will be privileged to help.

Food for the Hungry

As the disciples increased in numbers, and opposition to the faith increased, hunger got worse. The widows of the Greek-speaking believers were being neglected in the distribution of food. Seven were chosen to evenly distribute the food, and in this endeavor the word of God continued to spread (Acts 6:7). Later, the prophet Agabus said that there would be a great famine all

---

4. Hengel, *Property and Riches*, 34.
5. Hengel, *Property and Riches*, 42.
6. Hengel, *Property and Riches*, 44.

over the world. Adolf Schlatter wrote of these times, "Love embraced all man's concerns, bread as well as prayer, repentance as well as he knowledge of God."[7] Then the disciples determined that they would send relief to the believers living in Judea (Acts 11:28–30). In their meeting with Paul, the leaders of the Jerusalem church asked Paul and his new gentile converts to remember the poor, which Paul was eager to do (Gal 2:10).

Food and water were part of Paul's preaching. Speaking to the gentiles in the city of Lystra, Paul said, "In the past generations he allowed all the nations to follow their own ways. Yet he has not left himself without witness in doing good — giving your rains from heaven and fruitful seasons and filling you with food and your hearts with joy" (Acts 14:15–17). In addition to the bounty of God's creation in supplying food and water, Christians were urged to help. James warns, "If a brother or sister is naked and lacks daily food, and one of you says to them, 'Go in peace; keep warm and eat your fill,' and yet you do not supply their bodily needs, what is the good of that? So, faith by itself if it has no works, is dead" (Jas 2:4–17).

Even in the conflicts of the Corinthian congregation, Paul instructed them all to contribute to the saints in Jerusalem. He wrote, "On the first day of every week, each of you is to put aside and save whatever extra you earn, so that the collections need not be taken when I come. And when I arrive, I will send any whom you approve with letters to take your gift to Jerusalem" (1 Cor 16:1–3). As we will see later, this may have been the chief purpose for a collection since the congregation probably had no paid clergy.

Healing the Sick and Raising the Dead

Healing was also part of the good news of the Kingdom. Peter spoke to a crippled beggar, lame from birth, and said, "stand up and walk" (Acts 3:6). Many signs and wonders were done among the people by the apostles (Acts 5:12). Again, Peter in Lydda found a man named Aeneas, who had been bed ridden for eight years, and said, "Aeneas, Jesus Christ heals you, get up and make your bed" (Acts 9:32–34). In the pattern of Jesus, the Kingdom church even raises people from the dead. As widows showed the clothes that Dorcas had made, Peter said, "Tabitha, get up" (Acts 9:40). God also did extraordinary miracles through Paul (Acts 19:11), even raising from the dead a young man who fell asleep and fell during one of Paul's sermons (Acts 20:10).

---

7. Schlatter, *Church in the New Testament Period*, 26.

These miraculous healings called attention to the nearness of the Kingdom in the actions and world of the apostles as they did to Christ. In the Roman Empire there were no hospitals. The emperor and the upper class had private physicians, but the common people had little care other than questionable wandering physicians, magicians, and astrologers.[8] Duly noting the miracles of healing, Luke, both author and physician, like Christians throughout the ages, also used the practice of medicine to bring healing to the sick. To this day, God's Kingdom people bring healing both through prayers for the miraculous as well as the application of the medical arts.

Liberation of Prisoners

One of Isaiah's promises of the coming Kingdom that Jesus quoted in Nazareth was that he would proclaim liberty to the captives and release of the prisoners (Isa 61:1; Luke 4:18–21). The disciples were arrested and kept overnight for preaching that Jesus was the Messiah who was raised from the dead. Because of the pressure of the crowd, they were released the next day (Acts 4:21). After healing many and joining still others to the Lord, the apostles were arrested again. But during the night the angel of the Lord opened the prison door and let them out with the instruction that they should tell the people the whole message about this life (Acts 5:19–20). When he found out that it pleased many people, King Herod had James, the brother of John, killed. He also put Peter in prison. But again, an angel of the Lord brought him out of prison and described how the Lord had brought him out of prison (Acts 12:17).

For healing a slave girl who had the spirit of divination, her owners, losing their source of income, had Paul and Silas beaten and thrown in prison. About midnight, there was a violent earthquake that opened the gates of the prison. Staying where they were, Paul had opportunity to tell the jailer to believe on the Lord Jesus Christ for salvation. The next morning, they were released by the magistrate and received their apology (Acts 16:39). Even under house arrest in Rome, guarded by a soldier, Paul had the freedom to speak about Jesus and proclaim the Kingdom of God with all boldness and without hindrance (Acts 28:16–31).

The liberation of Hebrew slaves was to take place after seven years (Exod 21:2). If a slave ran away from his master, the person receiving the

---

8. Koester, *History, Culture, and Religion*, 317.

slave would not have to return him to his owner (Deut 23:15). Accordingly, Paul did not have to return Onesimus to his master but could have kept him in Rome as a helper. But Paul sent him back. Schlatter writes, "Christianity did not exist to change conditions by violence, but to permeate the old order by the new . . . Paul sent Onesimus back to Philemon (Phil 1:1), and in so doing he totally transcended the Roman norm of such relationships by this new factor of fellowship between master and man in the Christian community."[9]

Reconciliation of Diverse People

Another promise of the coming Kingdom would be that swords would be beaten into plowshares and that people would not learn war anymore (Mic 4:3). But for that to happen there would need to be a reconciliation of diverse people. Philipp, one of those chosen to help feed the hungry, went to alien Samaritans and proclaimed Jesus as the Messiah. Later he was sent to a road to answer questions asked by an Ethiopian treasurer. Receiving the good news with joy, he was baptized and made a participant in the Kingdom (Acts 8:4–39). Included also was an erstwhile enemy, a Roman centurion, whom Peter baptized (Acts 10:47). Gentiles were glad when they heard the word of the Lord (Acts 13:48). Other new believers were Dionysius, the Areopagite, and a woman named Damaris (Acts 17:33).

To many in the Jewish community, such diversity was an assault on their expectations. In their apocalyptic view of history, the chosen people within the nation of Israel would be saved in the final revelation. This view was shared by the Essenes and the Pharisees as well as those who had supported the Maccabean Revolt.[10] It is also a pointed rebuttal of nations that use religion to support their own policies. These include anti-refugee sentiments, terrorism against religious minorities, and interstate wars. In Christ there was a new identity. As Paul said so eloquently, "there is no longer Jew or Greek, there is no longer slave or free, there is no longer male and female; for all of you are one in Christ Jesus" (Gal 3:28).

---

9. Schlatter, *Church in the New Testament Period*, 221.
10. Koester, *History, Culture, and Religion*, 219–23.

DEFIANCE OF AUTHORITY

Within the prophetic tradition the good news of the coming Kingdom was always at odds with the unholy alliance between the rulers of the state and the institutional religion. This was true at the time of Jeremiah and Amos; it was also true in the early church. Schlatter wrote, "A movement which attached so much importance to the resurrection and the miraculous power of God was to the Sadducean rationalism, a dangerous menace ... Further, the disciples' messianic beliefs must inevitably lead, like the claims of Jesus himself, to a conflict with Rome."[11]

This is also true today. Organized religion benefits from the state if they do little to criticize the crimes of the rulers and injustice within society. This is how the Sadducees prospered in Jerusalem and why they feared the accusation of their involvement in the crucifixion and the good news of Jesus' resurrection. When that message was coupled with the feeding of the poor and the healing of the sick and lame, the messengers had to be suppressed (Acts 5:27).

Setting an example for the Kingdom church for all time, Peter and the apostles replied, "We must obey God rather than men" (Acts 5:29). This was not only a cry for freedom to tell the Christian message, but it was also an indictment of the Sadducees' collaboration with the Romans in the unjust murder of an innocent man for "religious reasons" (Acts 5:30). Coming out of a synagogue, members attacked Stephen for his wisdom and spirit and brought him before the council. After showing how Christ was foreshadowed and spoken of in the Scriptures, Stephen warned those of the religious rulers that they were the descendants of those who had killed the prophets who had foretold the coming of the Christ (Acts 7:52–53). In the midst of crises, the Kingdom church went against the authorities, the culture, the traditions, and even the moral law as it was understood at that time. Yet, perhaps more than any other book on the mission of the church, the book of Acts provides an exquisite pattern for evangelism and church life today.

---

11. Koester, *History, Culture, and Religion*, 84.

Chapter 6

The Kingdom in Crises

LITTLE CHILDREN ARE KILLED in a school shooting again. Tornados devastate towns in an eighty-mile rampage and climate change is blamed. Refugees by the thousands cross rivers and seas for jobs and homes. Two more nations close the door to democracy as they adopt authoritarian policies. Billions are spent on rockets and naval exercises while thousands starve. Problems have always existed but now they are qualitatively different. The frequency and severity of our crises signal a gigantic change in the world's system.

It happened before at the fall of the Roman Empire. It also took place when new nation-states, fueled by capitalism, separated themselves from the church. In each of these historical events, the Kingdom of God became a touchstone of how people could address the crises and live through them. As we examine this more closely, we can learn how it can do so again today.

THE FALL OF ROME AND AUGUSTINE

When Rome fell, it all but ended the imperial system in the Western world. That system began with the Assyrian Empire, followed by that of Babylon. The Persian Empire came next, followed by that of Greece. In many ways, Roman rule was the greatest achievement with civilization and an uneven peace spreading from Egypt to Scotland. Then, in 410, Alaric and the Visigoths sacked Rome. This was the beginning of events leading to the fall of Rome in 476. Though the empire was to continue in the East, Roman rule in the West decayed and declined. Invasions from Germanic and Eastern tribes swept through previously imperial territory. Legions were withdrawn from Britain. Seeking safety, slaves and freedmen gathered around villas, where they would work for a local lord. Soon the arteries of commerce and shipping lanes for grain were interrupted and ultimately lost.[1]

Some blamed the fall of Rome on the Christian faith. In the *City of God* St. Augustine refutes that argument and, in effect, refers to the Kingdom of God as an alternate political model. At one point he identifies the Kingdom of God with the city of God, the subject of his work. He writes, "There are so many things concerning Christ and the Kingdom of heaven, which is the city of God."[2] Quoting Psalms, he praises the city of God: "Glorious things are spoken of you, O city of God" (Ps 87:3). "Great is the LORD and greatly to be praised in the city of our God" (Ps 48:1). "Great is the LORD and greatly to be praised in the city of our God" (Ps 46:4). Augustine then compares the city of God with the city of man. In contrast to the city of God, the citizens of the earthly city prefer their own gods, impious and proud gods eager to grasp their own private privileges and seek divine honors from their deluded subjects.[3]

Augustine here made a sharp break with classical political theory. Plato and Aristotle spoke about the desirability of perfect human justice, but, at the same time, its practical impossibility. This suggested, at least implicitly, the need to supplement human justice with a higher and more genuine form of justice.[4] For Augustine, man's salvation, including his political salvation, accrues to him not from philosophy, as Plato thought, but through divine grace. Grace, rather than human justice, is what holds society together and is the source of true happiness.[5]

Influenced by the events of World War II and the Great Depression, political theorists like Reinhold Niebuhr, Hannah Arendt, and others saw in Augustine's view of politics a pessimistic realism. Much of their observations were based upon chapters 19 and 20 of the *City of God*. There Augustine speaks about the evils of the earthly city, the ugly realities of war, and his alternative definition of a commonwealth. A focus on these chapters for an understanding of Augustine's political thought produce a narrow focus on darker passages and an exaggerated emphasis of Augustine's pessimism.[6]

---

1. Starr, *History of the Ancient World*, 696–703.
2. Augustine, *City of God*, 514.
3. Augustine, *City of God*, 310–11.
4. Strauss and Cropsey, *History of Political Philosophy*, 156–57.
5. Strauss and Cropsey, *History of Political Philosophy*, 158.
6. Lamb, *Commonwealth of Hope*, 4–6.

By looking at Augustine's other writings and letters a new interpretation of Augustine's political thought is emerging. Delving more deeply into Augustine's definition of hope, citizens with diverse loves and different faiths can come together and decide upon the goods of civic peace and the ordered concord of the political community.[7] This is where the city of God can bring some of its insights and power into the city of men. Augustine also did not confine his view of politics just to government. His was a more expansive view. Rather than seeing politics just as reference to a state with laws, processes, and procedures, Augustine posited a commonwealth as a broader realm where citizens pursue temporal goods in common.[8]

Despite the realities of evil in politics, Augustine did not encourage political passivity or pessimism. Although he recognized that politics is intertwined by dangers, toils, and snares, he believed that seeking peace in the commonwealth can be a way of participating in the eternal city. Nor did he confine God's kingdom to the institutional church. He also valued the friendship of citizens who held different ultimate ends.[9]

SIGNS OF THE KINGDOM

As the props of Roman civilization were giving way, Augustine pointed to some of the positives of the Kingdom of God. He pointed out that normally when a city is sacked, no quarter is to given to the conquered. However, in the devastation of Rome, Alaric and the Visigoths were merciful to all who took refuge in the Christian churches.[10] Augustine also pointed out how society benefits from having a Christian ruler. The real happiness of such an emperor does not rest on a long life or defeat on enemies. Rather, it comes from ruling justly, remaining humble, and remembering that they are but servants of God. As such, they should be slow to punish and ready to pardon.[11]

From his letters as a bishop, Augustine also came out strongly against torture and the death penalty. He voiced strong opposition to torture at a time when it was widely accepted. He said that it offended him and his way of thinking. In other letters he implored Roman officials to avoid using

---

7. Lamb, *Commonwealth of Hope*, 198.
8. Lamb, *Commonwealth of Hope*, 270.
9. Lamb, *Commonwealth of Hope*, 201.
10. Augustine, *City of God*, 8–9.
11. Augustine, *City of God*, 159.

torture as a way of interrogation and instead encouraging them to be merciful and set an example of Christian gentleness. He also came out firmly against the death penalty. For him, the finality of the death penalty prevents any possibility for repentance and reform. In another letter he wrote, "we do not ask for vengeance on our enemies on this earth . . . We love our enemies and pray for them . . . That is why we desire their reform and not their deaths."[12]

Perhaps most significant was that Augustine's *City of God* was to set a new pattern of the Kingdom of God to have precedence over the earthly kingdom of men. As Rome weakened and its rulers faded under pressure, catholic popes became both spiritual and at times temporal leaders of society. When Rome was threatened by the Attila the Hun, Pope Leo I went to meet him and persuaded him not to attack the city.[13] His successor, Pope Gregory I, took on the responsibility to keep Rome fed. He also managed the estates of the church so successfully that revenues were increased, and workers were treated more humanely.[14]

If the city of God was to take precedence over the city of men, who should represent God's Kingdom? With a decaying empire and a strong, organized, and energized church, popes and bishops took the crown with what developed as their own armies, territories, and jurisdictions. Not long after, Charlemagne and his descendants were inspired by Augustine to construct a social philosophy to make their realm the City of God.[15] Later these two views would collide in the tensions between popes and emperors.

Apart from Augustine, two other features of the Kingdom of God were important when Rome fell. One was that early Christians disagreed with the Graeco-Roman world's participation in war. No Christian literature in the first three centuries of Christianity condoned a Christian's participation in war. Tertullian argued against Christians serving in Roman armies because it meant being under a master who was not Christ. While some Christians might serve in police functions, they frowned on serving in time of war.[16]

The other aspect of the Kingdom that produced home, work, food, healing, and education was the monasteries. With worship at its core and agriculture providing self-sufficiency, monasteries sought to preserve

12. Lamb, *Commonwealth of Hope*, 208, 209.
13. Fitzpatrick, "Leo the Great versus Attila the Hun"
14. Latourette, *History of Christianity*, 338.
15. Latourette, *History of Christianity*, 355.
16. Latourette, *History of Christianity*, 242–43.

and propagate learning. Monasteries provided healthcare and aid for the outcasts of society. Through their hospitals they also supplied aid for the orphaned and poor and even fed prisoners.[17] Through all these activities they announced by words and actions that the Kingdom of God was at hand.

When Rome fell and a whole civilization was threatened, St. Augustine spoke of how the city of God not only endured but provided the pattern for life on this world. His political theory looked realistically at the injustices and evils of government. Yet it also opened the possibility of good rulers, be they pope or emperor. In the face of devastation and carnage Christians protected the vulnerable, fed the poor, refused to go to war, and created institutions that healed the sick, educated the young, and promoted scholarship and learning. However, in the succeeding centuries, Christians themselves would succumb to the temptations of all governments, whether they be the papacy, the empire, or monasteries. Yet the Kingdom lived on.

LUTHER AND TWO KINGDOMS?

For a thousand years the *City of God* helped to shape the Western world. It was an uneasy synthesis between church and secular authorities. Yet it provided a general unity of faith and culture for an entire civilization. The Kingdom of God had not only outlasted the Roman Empire but provided some of the ideals of the society that followed. Every era, however, has an end as well as a beginning. The late Middle Ages experienced several shocks that changed the course of history. Politically, the Holy Roman Empire, largely ruled by the Hohenstaufens and later the Hapsburgs, had weakened, and territories within Germany and its neighbors had become much stronger.[18]

In 1519 Charles V became emperor and almost immediately had to contend with a war with France. France was by this time a formidable power. To counter France, Charles made a pact with Henry VIII in England, now a much more powerful king in England. Then, with his troops complaining that they had not been paid, Charles's troops assaulted Rome with terrifying results. Not long after, the Turks invaded Austria and Hungary

---

17. Latourette, *Thousand Years of Uncertainty*, 38, 364–66.
18. Reinhardt, *Germany 2000 Years*, 162–74.

and surrounded Vienna.[19] Though Charles was victorious over the Turks at that battle, the medieval synthesis was disintegrating.

Another shock to the medieval system was the new learning of the Renaissance and humanism. In the late Middle Ages questions about authority, truth, and the best method for knowing were being asked.[20] Questions even arose about the authority and legitimacy of the pope's temporal authority as scholars questioned the truthfulness of a document called *On the Donation of Constantine*.[21] With the new learning came new questions. The whole intellectual value system that supported the medieval synthesis between the Christian faith and Western civilization was unraveling.

According to William Wright, the roots of Luther's concept of the two kingdoms were in his quest for the certainty of knowing. Luther discovered that the Word of God brought its own certainty through faith. This was the language of the heart and provided the certainty of salvation. That was the base on which all Christian instruction was built. This knowledge was different from that which was arrived at through reason. Government uses human reason to rule effectively. As a result, there is a qualitative difference between the assurance of salvation and the quest for a more just society.[22]

As Augustine separated the city of God from the earthly city, Luther separated the Kingdom of God's grace and love from the kingdom of secular authority based on law and reason. Yet at the same time he opposed what history had done with Augustine's preference of the sacred over the secular. Addressing that mixture of the two at his time, he complained that "bishops, instead of governing souls with the Word, 'rule castles, cities, lands, and people outwardly.' And the secular authorities . . . wish to exercise a spiritual rule over souls, prescribing the papist faith and trying to root out the Lutheran heresy by force."[23]

For Luther, there are two types of rule. There is the uncoercive Word of God in the church and the legal, coercive rule of government. Both are governments of God but only to the secular authority has he given the right to punish and the right to go to war. In the spiritual government the Holy Spirit produces Christians. In the temporal he restrains the wicked so that

---

19. Schwiebert, *Luther and His Times*, 49–64.
20. Wright, *Martin Luther's Understanding of God's Two Kingdoms*, 46.
21. Wright, *Martin Luther's Understanding of God's Two Kingdoms*, 96.
22. Wright, *Martin Luther's Understanding of God's Two Kingdoms*, 12–14.
23. Bornkamm, *Luther's Doctrine of the Two Kingdoms*, 6.

they are obliged to keep the peace. These two governments belong together, and the Christian will live within both of them.[24]

THE LEGACY OF LUTHER'S TWO KINGDOMS

For the general public, one legacy of Luther's two-kingdoms theory is the separation of church and state. For historians and theologians, however, this legacy fails to capture what Luther was really saying. Nevertheless, the concept has been so politicized as to become a political teaching. One interpretation of the two kingdoms is that the temporal government, governed by nature and reason, is autonomous and is free from God's revealed law. Indeed, God's will is evident in nature and reason, but it does not depend on any special revelation from God's Word. Following this line of thought, another commentator identified Luther's teaching with Machiavelli, who reasoned that the state must govern according to its own self-interest. Even though Luther never asserted that the state must preserve itself and promote its welfare above all things, some read this into the two-kingdoms teaching.[25]

The rise of Naziism in Germany provided a new context for applying the autonomy of the state and the worldly spheres of life. The perverted use of the two-kingdoms doctrine by the Nazis and their collaborating German Christians caused a lot of questioning about the value of the teaching by Lutherans themselves. Using the ideas of *volk* and racial distinctions as "timeless" orders of the worldly sphere, they totally obliterated what Luther taught about God's work through the state. It was the national socialists that made gods out of the state, war, nation, and race.[26]

The two-kingdoms doctrine was a theme in the German church struggle against Naziism. Those opposing Hitler articulated the original Lutheran idea that all Christians must obey Christ and that the state is to provide justice and peace. The independent Lutheran church in Hesse spoke to the Nazi regime and declared that "they had recognized only Christ as their head and king and Christ would remain their king." They would continue to do this despite a call for loyalty to one man, or a king, or a state, or as a *volk*, or a majority, or a race, or anything else at all.[27]

---

24. Bornkamm, *Luther's Doctrine of the Two Kingdoms*, 8.
25. Wright, *Martin Luther's Understanding of God's Two Kingdoms*, 17–27.
26. Wright, *Martin Luther's Understanding of God's Two Kingdoms*, 31.
27. Wright, *Martin Luther's Understanding of God's Two Kingdoms*, 32–33.

Partially because of its misuse by the Nazi regime, and even more by a rejection of the dualism it implied, the two-kingdoms teaching was rejected by some, including Dietrich Bonhoeffer, a Lutheran, who wrote, "This division of the whole of reality into the sacred and profane, Christian and worldly, sectors creates the possibility of existence in only one of these sectors: for instance, a spiritual existence that takes no part in the worldly existence, and a worldly existence that can make good its autonomy over against the sacred sector."[28] While the Middle Ages elevated the spiritual realm over the worldly, Bonhoeffer observed that the modern age is characterized by the ever-progressing independence of the secular over the spiritual. For Bonhoeffer, there is only one reality. That reality is revealed in Christ in the reality of the world. "The world has no reality of its own independent of God's revelation in Christ. It is a denial of God's revelation in Jesus Christ to wish to be Christian, without being 'worldly.'"[29]

Both Luther and Augustine addressed the crises of their times with reference to the Kingdom of God. Their times were different as was their application of Jesus' teaching to the world in which they lived. Augustine addressed a civilization that was falling apart but, in the Christian faith, was being reborn. Luther struggled for fresh air in a closed society. Each of them made important contributions to political theory. Augustine's legacy was that politics has its limits. There still is hope but it comes from the grace of God. Luther's lasting contribution was that faith should avoid the sword and the state should not use religion for its own ends. As the world faces contemporary crises, it will be tempted, as Bonhoeffer warned, to champion the independence of the secular over the spiritual. That is the way of death. Needed is a new political theory of the Kingdom of God that can steer the world to a better future until Christ comes again. Any new political theory based on the Kingdom will need to address the crises of capitalism and nationalism that are challenging the present world system.

---

28. Bonhoeffer, *Ethics*, 57.
29. Bonhoeffer, *Ethics*, 57–58.

Chapter 7

Good News in Trying Times

THE MODERN WORLD HAS BROUGHT unprecedented prosperity and security to a growing number of the world's people. However, it has done so, in part, through exploitation, enslavement, robbery, genocide, and the destruction of wildlife and the environment. Wars have slain millions; hunger and preventable illness have killed even more. Current threats to the economy and to the nation-state system are bringing back some of the fears of former years. Yet, as we shall see, even in trying times Christ has blessed the whole world with the gifts of the Kingdom.

CHRIST'S KINGDOM

Unlike the view in the Middle Ages, Christ's Kingdom is much broader than the church or even the church-blessed monarchs. Christ was in the beginning with God. All things came into being through him and without him not one thing came into being (John 1:3). Paul writes, "In him all things in heaven and earth were created . . . whether thrones, dominions or powers—all things were created through him and for him" (Col 1:16). Christ's power is also a work in progress. "Through him God was pleased to reconcile to himself all things, whether on earth or in heaven, by making peace through the blood of his cross" (Col 1:20).

This means that Christ's Kingdom grows in many ways. In the light of the cosmic Christ, nothing is secular. The blessings of God's New World Society come through elections, political parties, and nongovernmental organizations as well as though saints, missionaries, church charities, and prayers. Given the power of the world economy and the control of nations, even the partial realization of a New World Society seems hopeless. Yet, Jesus' miracles were the invitation to hope. From his miracles of healing came a multitude of hospitals, Christian, Jewish, and public. His feeding of thousands has inspired Christians to support food banks and aid convoys that have fed millions. His crossing of national and cultural boundaries has led to international understanding and peace-making.

In more contemporary times God has worked through people to bring about the blessings of the Kingdom. Some of them have come from Christian churches, others from governments, still others from civil society. Yet in their words and work they changed the course of history to bring about the signs of God's New World Society.

MODERATING COLONIALISM AND ITS LEGACY

The crimes of colonialism have been some of the most terrible in history. When greed merged with national imperialism, entire peoples were destroyed. Others were enslaved. Rationales were given that colonization was for the spread of the Christian faith and civilization. Europeans would make better use of the land and develop the natural resources of the conquered land for the benefit of humanity. But to accomplish this the land was stolen, the natives were killed, and diseases spread.

One who protested the colonial carnage in Latin America was the Dominican priest Bartolomé de las Casas. Traveling between the New World and Spain many times, he argued against the *encomienda* system.[1] This was the promise of free land stolen from the natives, which would be given to the settler, as well as the forced labor of the natives who had once lived on the land. De las Casas also sought to improve the life of miners who produced the coveted gold and silver. Days off, rest periods, no child workers, and time off to work on their farms were his demands.[2] He attacked the *Conquistadores*' use of the just war theory to justify the slaughter of the natives. Instead, he cited the just war theory to justify the first peoples' fighting to protest their land from the colonizers.[3]

Inspired by de las Casas, some five hundred years later, Gustavo Gutierrez would write a book about him, entitled *Las Casas: In Search of the*

---

1. Olique, ed., *Bertolomé de las Casas*, 85–86.
2. Olique, ed., *Bartolomé de las Casas*, 160–61.
3. Olique, ed., *Bartolomé de las Casas*, 220–41.

Poor of Jesus Christ.[4] Gutierrez, the dean of liberation theologians, wrote *A Theology of Liberation*. For Gutierrez, "the elimination of misery and exploitation is sign of the coming of the Kingdom. It will become a reality, according to the book of Isaiah, when there is happiness and rejoicing among the people because 'men shall build houses and live to inhabit them, plant vineyards and eat their fruit; they shall not build for others to inhabit nor plant for others to eat'"[5]

Although liberation theology was criticized by the Vatican under Pope John Paul for its use of Marxist analysis to describe the effects of colonialism in Latin America, its results have been far reaching. In the twenty-first century democratic leftist leaders have come to power in Brazil, Argentina, Ecuador, Bolivia, Chile, and Columbia. Some were replaced for a while only to be replaced by others of the center/left parties. Even more important was the election of Pope Francis in 2013. While not an advocate of the Marxist framework some used in liberation theology, his concern for the poor, the disabled, and refugees around the world have made a profound impression and difference in world affairs.

THE DEATH KNELL OF SLAVERY

A friend of William Pitt, well-to-do, and a respected member of the British Parliament, William Wilberforce, like many in his position, enjoyed the pleasures of his class. Then, on a trip to Europe with an evangelical mentor, he started reading the New Testament in Greek. Gradually Wilberforce came to see that he needed to change his life. A movement for the abolition of slavery, led by the Quakers, was already in existence. Moved by his newfound evangelical faith and exposed to the evils of slavery, Wilberforce used his position in Parliament to end the slave trade.[6]

It was a lifelong struggle against the vested interests of slave traders and owners. There were many delays and defeats because of the mounting resistance to any moves to threaten profits. Yet, because of the pressures of the abolitionists and the skill of Wilberforce and his allies in Parliament, a bill was passed ending the slave trade in 1809.[7] However, it was just the beginning of the actual end of the slave trade. In 1839 Britain had treaties

---

4. Gutierrez, *Las Casas*.
5. Gutierrez, *Theology of Liberation*, 167, quoting Isaiah 65:21–22.
6. Tomkins, *William Wilberforce*, 36–53.
7. Tomkins, *William Wilberforce*, 167.

that allowed them to seize slave ships still operating. Then came the question of slavery itself. Would slaves get their freedom? Two days before Wilberforce died, Britain ended slavery in 1831. France released its slaves in 1848 and the US freed its slaves in 1863.[8] The world had practiced slavery in every empire and every nation until these momentous events. However, coming out of the faith of leaders like Wilberforce and countless others in the abolitionist movements, slavery was on the way out. As the prophets had promised and Jesus proclaimed, "The Lord has anointed me; he has sent me to bring good news to the oppressed, to bind up the brokenhearted, to proclaim liberty to the captives" (Isa 61:1; Luke 4:18).

Though the slave trade ended, segregation and discrimination against former slaves has continued. In 1967 half of all African Americans lived in substandard housing; they had half the income of whites. Twice as many were unemployed. Infant mortality was double that of whites. Segregated schools received less money per student as did white schools. Of employed blacks, 75 percent held menial jobs.[9] Segregation in the American South was codified into law. On buses whites would sit in front and blacks in the rear. The whites were afraid that a Black man would accidentally rub knees with a white woman.[10] After Rosa Parks refused to give up her seat, she was arrested. This sparked outrage in the Black community and African Americans organized to protest. Martin Luther King Jr. was elected to provide leadership in the Black boycott of buses in Montgomery, Alabama.[11]

Acting out of his Christian faith and concerned for the liberation of the descendants of slaves, King stressed that the image of God is shared by all people. Therefore, the worth of every individual does not lie in his intellect, his racial origin, or his social position. "An individual has value because he has value with God."[12] With this as a guiding star, King and other Christians, Jews, and others, Black and white, worked to end segregation and gain civil rights for African Americans in the United States. Yet it was only a beginning. African Americans continue to suffer and lag behind their fellow Americans in jobs, income, healthcare, and education. More needs to be done.

8. Tomkins, *William Wilberforce*, 218–22.
9. King, *Where Do We Go from Here?*, 7.
10. Branch, *Parting the Waters*, 146.
11. Branch, *Parting the Waters*, 137.
12. King, *Where Do We Go from Here?*, 102–3.

Good News in Trying Times

REDUCING POVERTY AND HUNGER

In 1997 42 percent of the population of India and China lived in extreme poverty.[13] In 1964 and 1965 India received five million tons of wheat from America and some from Canada and Australia.[14] Norman Borlaug, a Christian from Iowa, helped to develop a Mexican wheat and crossed it with varieties from India and Pakistan. When these new varieties were used with fertilizer and increased irrigation water supplies, it enabled farmers to grow two or three crops a year. Production in some areas increased 400 percent.[15] In 1968 Pakistan became self-sufficient in grain and India did as well several years later.[16] In the Asian subcontinent, this green revolution has helped to feed millions and enabled India and Pakistan to feed their own people and export wheat to other nations. In 2021–2022 India exported 7.68 million tons of wheat.[17]

China's "economic miracle," ameliorating poverty and hunger, had its beginnings in a secret visit by Henry Kissinger to the Chinese Premier Chou En-Lai in 1971. Negotiations took place inviting President Nixon to China and opened China to better relations with the United States and the world.[18] In the succeeding years, largely under the leadership of Deng Xiaoping, joint ventures with foreign capital and expertise led to the massive industrialization of the country. By 1987, ten thousand Chinese were studying in America and since then more than two million Chinese have been educated in the US.[19] With open access to markets in the US and Southeast Asia, millions of Chinese were better fed and lifted from poverty. As God chose Cyrus, the emperor of Persia, to release the Jews to go back to their homeland (Isa 45:13), now the blessings of God's Kingdom came through the leadership of a Jewish diplomat and communist rulers.

---

13. Rosling, *Factfulness*, 53.

14. Hesser, *Man Who Fed the World*, 79.

15. This writer participated in the "Pakistan Project" at Colorado State University, 1968–1970, where six departments of the university contributed their expertise to the green revolution in Pakistan, and authored a study, *Water Management in West Pakistan*.

16. Hesser, *Man Who Fed the World*, 100.

17. Bhardwaj, "India's Wheat Exports," 1.

18. Isaacson, *Kissinger*, 341–47.

19. Pomfret, *Beautiful Country and the Middle Kingdom*, 490–95.

The Last Kingdom Standing

PATHS TO PEACE

Though wars abound, the paths to peace are rare. Yet, when they occur, they provide lessons for other conflicts. Two examples from Africa provide some hope for the future. The eastern region of Nigeria, called Biafra, sought to secede from the nation. Partially fueled by oil revenues, it was able to hold off federal forces for some time. In the conflict an estimated million or more people died. Near the end of the war, a missionary was traveling through Lagos and at his hotel was abruptly summoned to meet with Major Gowan, then commander of the federal forces. Gowan told the missionary that the war would be ending in several weeks, but he wanted to tell another Christian what would happen. Because he was a Christian, he would not prosecute the leaders of the rebellion. Instead, he would welcome back the rebels and work out some political solutions to avoid such rebellions leading to war in the future.[20] Soon thereafter, the nation was divided into states, preventing a repeat of an entire region seceding from the country.

In South Africa the World Council of Churches contributed to the prevention of what might have been the worst of the civil wars of Africa. This would have been between Black Africans and the white ruling regime. Through the Programme to Combat Racism (PCR) grants were made to the liberation movements in Southern Africa. They were given for humanitarian aid but were quickly criticized for helping to arm so-called terrorists in the liberation struggles.[21] In addition, the PCR asked member churches to divest from South Africa. It also published the names of all transnational corporations involved in the apartheid state and urged them to divest.[22] In South Africa Archbishop Desmond Tutu advocated widespread sanctions, citing that they were the only means of avoiding a bloody conflict in the nation.[23]

With widespread divestment and the fall of the South African currency, negotiations began with the leaders of the African National Congress (ANC). Prompted by the resilience of the liberation movements, the struggle of many whites against apartheid, and a falling economy, Nelson Mandela was released from prison, elections were held, and war was averted. Perhaps

---

20. Interview with Rev. Paul Volz, St. Louis, circa 1968.
21. Schmidt, "Legitimacy of Revolution," 292.
22. Schmidt, "Legitimacy of Revolution," 191–92.
23. Welsh, *Rise and Fall of Apartheid*, 237.

just as important was the creation of the Truth and Reconciliation Commission (TRC), headed by Archbishop Tutu. Under this commission the crimes of both the white government forces as well as those of the liberation movements were revealed so that some reconciliation could take place between the sides that had been alienated for centuries.[24] Working through church organizations, secular leaders of corporations, conscience-stricken citizens, and the demands of revolutionaries, some of the blessings of this New World Society were realized.

HEALTH AND HEALING

The most dramatic and persuasive signs of the nearness of the Kingdom in Jesus' day were his miracles of healing. Then near the end of his life he said, "Very truly, I tell you, the one who believes in me will also do the works that I do and, in fact, will do greater works than these, because I am going to the father" (John 14:12). Peter healed a lame man (Acts 3:6). Paul commanded a man to walk who had been crippled from birth (Acts 14:19). In some cases of emergency, miracles still happen. Yet, it has been in the creation of hospitals and clinics throughout the world that the blessings of the Kingdom in health and healing have been so impressive. In many of the poorer nations of the world the first hospitals were formed in the name of Christ. Even today hospitals retain biblical or denominational names even though they are largely run by corporations or the government.

Even more significant has been the development of vaccines and medicines that have ended or severely limited some the world's worst scourges. Smallpox is finished. Modern-day leprosy (Hansen's disease) has largely been cured.[25] As scientists and physicians have worked on vaccines and cures, the list of diseases that have been nearly eliminated is simply staggering: plague, polio, measles, yellow fever, rubella, tetanus, mumps, chickenpox, and diphtheria. Now across the whole world 88 percent of all one-year-olds had received at least one vaccination by 2016. Globally,

---

24. Welsh, *Rise and Fall of Apartheid*, 570.

25. It was my privilege to have served in Nigeria, where fellow missionary Dr. Bill Foege was one of the those who helped develop the strategy to eliminate smallpox. There I also visited a ruined leprosaria, which was no longer needed because the disease was under control in the entire region.

children dying before their fifth birthday has gone from about 40 percent in 1900 to about 4 percent in 2016.[26]

The recent COVID pandemic demonstrates that even as yesterday's diseases are quashed, new diseases come to take their place. In addition, some of the most severe, such as cancer, heart disease, and malaria, continue to take their toll. Yet even with these diseases the promise is there for finding cures, or at least strategies to prolong life. In health and healing the Kingdom is near enough to bring hope and solace to those who need it most.

FORGIVENESS AND DEATH'S END

The forgiveness of sins and the good news of the resurrection in Christ is now being heard and believed throughout the world. Though the church in Western Europe and the United States is in decline, in the rest of the world it is growing. Now, in Africa, 685 million people identify themselves as followers of Jesus. In Latin America the figure is 617 million. By the middle of the twenty-first century the total number of Christians in the world is expected to exceed 3.2 billion.[27] Christianity has seen its greatest growth in Africa, Latin America, and Asia. Christianity has now become the religion of the East and South.[28]

Why is it that the number of confessing Christians is declining in the West and growing elsewhere? Some put the blame on the Enlightenment and a more scientific understanding of the universe. Other cite the fact that while forgiveness in Christ and eternal life is new in other cultures, it is a tired and worn message in America and Europe. Perhaps even more significant is that in those areas where there has been explosive growth, the message of salvation is closely tied to the blessings of the Kingdom. In Ethiopia's fast-growing Mekane Yesus Church, the struggle for human rights is part of the good news of the gospel. "Holistic Theology" is seen as a critical approach to the church's teachings.[29] In Korea Christian social movement organizations worked tirelessly to attain democracy and human rights in South Korea.[30]

26. Rosling, *Factfulness*, 60–63.
27. Center for the Study of Global Christianity, "Status of Global Christianity, 2023."
28. Bays, *New History of Christianity in China*, 203.
29. Deressa, "Critical Approach," 153–69.
30. Buswell and Lee, *Christianity in Korea*, 200.

Christian missions, from their very beginning, created clinics, hospitals, and schools. In these places forgiveness and the hope of salvation was connected with healing and education. Together with these institutions there has been an exponential increase in Pentecostalism, which connects divine intervention with spiritual and physical healing. In China, this was very prominent in the 1980s, especially in rural areas.[31] Throughout Africa Neo-Pentecostalism has spread very rapidly, attracting youth through music and relevance in helping them get along in life.[32] The same is true in Latin America, where millions have left the Catholic Church for Pentecostalism. Attracted particularly by faith healing and a "prosperity gospel" promising financial success, the message is very appealing to those who have very little.[33] The forgiveness of sins and the promise of eternal life connected with the other promises of the Kingdom is very welcomed in areas of the world where the needs of people are the greatest.

God's New World Society, with its promises of food, water, liberation, healing, homes and jobs, peace, forgiveness, and eternal life, has partially been realized in recent history. Yet, today it is confronted with new crises to the capitalist economy and the nation-state system. Jesus proclaimed that the Kingdom was near even though days later he wept over the destruction of Jerusalem. Is he proclaiming the nearness of the Kingdom in the crises to come?

---

31. Bays, *New History of Christianity in China*, 194.
32. Bongmba, *Routledge Companion to Christianity in Africa*, 299.
33. Masci, "Why Has Pentecostalism Grown?"

Chapter 8

God's New World Society

THE KINGDOM OF GOD is for the whole world. When God promised to make of Abraham a great nation, all the nations of the earth would be blessed (Gen 12:3). "By his offspring shall all the nations of the earth gain blessings for themselves" (Gen 22:18). Picking up on these promises, the psalmist says, "You are my son; today I have begotten you. Ask of me, and I will make the nations your heritage, and the ends of the earth your possession" (Ps 2:8). And David sings, "The Lord is good to all, and his compassion is over all that he has made ... Your kingdom is an everlasting kingdom, and your dominion endures throughout all generations" (Ps 145:8–13).

As the Kingdom is for the whole world, Christ can use people from the whole world to bring it about. Though they are not Christians, many fear God and do what is right. As Peter said of Cornelius, an enemy commander from Rome, "God shows no partiality but that in every nation anyone who fears him and does what is right is acceptable to him" (Acts 10:34–35). As the heavens declare the glory of God, Paul asks, has not that voice of creation gone out to all the earth followed by simple human decency (Rom 10:18)?

As God measures the waters in the hollow of his hand and weighs the mountains in scales, all the nations are like a drop from a bucket (Isa 40:12–15). Christ came quietly with a God-sized task: "He will not cry or lift up his voice ... he will faithfully bring forth justice. He will not grow faint or be crushed until he has established justice in the earth (Isa 42:2, 3). And with justice also comes salvation: "I will give you as a light to the nations, that my salvation may reach to the end of the earth" (Isa 49:6). It is a Kingdom without borders.

What might be a phrase that communicates this worldwide Kingdom of God to people across the globe, many of whom are not Christian or even religious? One way to speak of this might be to call it "God's New World Society." As in the day of Jesus, it was not a new world "order" with the use of coercive force. Rather, it was a group of people with some shared values who, for the most part, have influenced the world for good.

When Jesus announced that the Kingdom of God was at hand, it was unbelievable until they saw his miracles and heard his message. Announcing that a New World Society is near today, at a time of climate change, failing states, dying refugees, polarized societies, and preparations for war, is equally unbelievable. Yet, today the good news is that Christ is now working through God's New World Society.

CHRISTIANS

Christians are often in the forefront as Christ's vehicles for bringing about the blessings of the Kingdom. Even though denominations and interdenominational groups have often differed widely in theology, governance, and politics, they have shown remarkable similarities in the ways in which they have sought to feed people, heal the sick, provide potable water, and work for better housing and peace between warring communities. Some of these efforts are through direct aid and others through their advocacy of programs and politics helping the most vulnerable. It has not gone unnoticed that by concentrating on helping the neediest, Christians discover the path to greater unity.

World Council of Churches

One of the preliminary groups to the World Council of Churches was the Life and Work Movement. This was an effort to bring together Protestants and some Orthodox from various nations and traditions who were working for similar goals. In Germany, Christian social ministry provided homes for epileptics, work colonies for the unemployed, and settlement houses. Similar actions were happening in America, England, and other nations.[1] Many working in these endeavors realized that charity alone could not fully deal with social evils. In England, Christian Socialists, rejecting Marxism,

---

1. Karlstrom, "Movements for International Friendship," 519.

helped to bring about the Christian Social Union. In Germany Adolf Harnack and others founded the Evangelisch Sozialer Kongress. Participants in both the charitable and political work observed that Christian social movements would become powerful factors in bringing about unity among Protestant churches.[2]

At a meeting of the Life and Work Conference in 1925, a message to the churches set forth a principle of Christian internationalism addressing the universal nature of the church, examining the problem of racism, and proposing an international order providing peaceful methods for averting the causes of war. A continuation committee was formed and established a center in Geneva, Switzerland. Later it would have contact with other Christians organizations, the League of Nations, and the International Labor Office, and became one of the pillars of the World Council of Churches.[3]

Many of the denominations in America that are part of the World Council of Churches have come to work together in the Church World Service (CWS). They have been especially active in working with migrants and refugees in Africa, Asia, and Latin America. In Kenya they support a camp that helps prepare migrants for life in the countries to which they may be traveling. In Central America they have established way stations for refugees fleeing north to the United States. In Asia, they have continued to work with some of the displaced people in Myanmar and Cambodia.

Evangelicals

Under the leadership of Billy Graham, some 2,700 Evangelicals from 150 countries met in Lausanne, Switzerland for an International Congress on World Evangelism. In North America evangelism was seen partly as a reaction to the liberal social gospel that defined many churches. However, at the International Congress, Latin Americans and Africans insisted that evangelization and mission must have a wide focus than on personal salvation. Some spoke on the need for a holistic mission that included advocacy and action to fight social injustice and serve the poor. They said that you cannot preach the gospel with credibility while ignoring the suffering of those to whom you preach. The necessity to bring together evangelism and social concern led to the creation of an ongoing structure. This led to

---

2. Karlstrom, "Movements for International Friendship," 509, 510.
3. Gaines, *World Council of Churches*, 50–51.

the Lausanne Committee for World Evangelization, which has worked in tandem with the older World Evangelical Alliance (WEA).[4]

Today the World Evangelical Alliance is a global association that serves six hundred million evangelicals worldwide. It is composed of evangelical alliances in seven regions and 129 nations. It is working in theological education, religious liberty, and social justice issues like human trafficking, poverty, peace-building, creation care, and nuclear weapons disarmament.[5] The WEA is represented at the UN and has increased its engagement to promote peace and reconciliation, help for the poor, and communicating evangelical beliefs and values. It also has task forces on "Care for Creation" and "Migration and Refugees."

Politically, evangelicals, like other religious groups, are divided. Some, like Ron Sider, quote the Scriptures to advocate "distributive justice." He points out that hundreds and hundreds of Bible verses speak about God's special concern for the poor and the oppressed and points out that self-proclaimed believers who do not share their possessions are not Christians at all.[6] On the other side many evangelicals have played an important role in conservative and Republican politics. In some cases, evangelical churches believe that they are in a position to win the so-called culture wars in America, elevating concerns about abortion and same-sex marriage over those dealing with refugees and the homeless.[7]

Evangelicals have been most successful in international aid through their work in World Vision. For decades WEA and World Vision have partnered in outreach bringing peace and wholeness to the world's most vulnerable children. World Vision has addressed the whole issue of global hunger and access to clean drinking water, especially as it affects children. Through the sponsorship of children and donations, World Vision deals with both emergency aid and also long-term development.

Roman Catholics

Among Roman Catholics, aid for the poor and vulnerable has become an overriding purpose for the church body, from sisters in Africa working in rural hospitals to Pope Francis making his first papal visit to weep over the

---

4. Dowsett, "Evangelicals and the Lausanne Movement," 58–60.
5. Stiller, "Introduction to the World Evangelical Alliance," 3.
6. Sider, "Evangelicals and Social Justice," 128–29.
7. Eskridge, "Evangelicals in North America," 309–11.

bodies of refugees who drowned seeking to come to Europe.[8] The tradition of welcoming those in need around the world dates to the earliest monasteries but has been updated to meet the challenges of inequality from feudalism to capitalism. Today's Vincent de Paul Society reflects their founder, a devout sixteenth-century priest who helped convince lords and ladies to share their wealth.[9] In America, Dorothy Day surprised her free-spirited friends and became a Roman Catholic. Inspired by her newfound faith and her hobo prophet, Peter Maurin, she published *The Catholic Worker*, addressing injustice, and served the victims of that injustice who came to her door for bread and soup.[10]

Around the world 162 national Catholic relief and development agencies operate under Caritas, centered in Rome. Founded in Germany in 1897 and renamed Caritas Internationalis in 1951, Caritas has a rich history of listening to the poor and giving them the tools to transform their lives. It is guided by the moral and spiritual principles of dignity, justice, solidarity, and stewardship.[11] The range of Caritas's presence and ability to help in times of crisis is truly remarkable. During an Argentinian political and economic collapse, every parish there had a Caritas office and the infrastructure to mount a major relief operation.[12]

While Protestants in England and Germany advocated for the disenfranchised by creating and joining socialist parties, Roman Catholics, operating from a larger base, formed their own social movement. In 1891 Pope Leo XIII wrote the encyclical *Rerum Novarum*. This supported the rights of labor to form unions. It rejected both socialism and unrestricted capitalism while affirming the right to private property. It has become the foundational text for modern Catholic social teaching.[13] However, from a developing world perspective, some Catholic theologians and activists did not believe it considered the political realities they saw around them. Gustavo Gutierrez writes that the major problem to be considered is how the Kingdom of God can be realized in the unjust structures of society, especially in Latin America.[14] In Medellin, Columbia, in 1968, a Council of

---

8. Inverleigh, *Great Reformer*, 1–3.
9. Forbes, *St. Vincent de Paul*, 26–30.
10. Mayfield, *Unruly Saint*, 119–30.
11. Caritas, https://www.caritas.org/who-we-are/.
12. Inverleigh, *Great Reformer*, 267.
13. Inverleigh, *Great Reformer*, 20.
14. Gutierrez, *Theology of Liberation*, 45–47.

Latin American Bishops expanded the Christian understanding of liberation as freedom not just from sin but also from sinful social structures. This was the origin of what came to be known as "liberation theology." On the continent, it gave the Church its own distinctive slogan as "the preferential option for the poor."[15]

Under the name of liberation theology, some adopted a Marxist framework in addressing the savage inequalities they saw around them. Others, like Archbishop Bergoglio, now Pope Francis, saw in the Marxist analysis an "adolescent progressivism" leading to a militant secularism in Venezuela and in Argentina under the Kirchners.[16] For the archbishop, his "preferential option for the poor" meant visiting them in the slums and listening to them spell out their faith and their remedies for society. By so doing, change would come not from a small group of activists but from the shared concerns of the entire community.[17]

Denominations

Some denominations not only work in umbrella associations but also have their own international programs. With support from people in Scandinavian countries, Germany, the United States, and other countries, Lutheran World Relief focuses on sustainable development projects and disaster relief and recovery. The United Methodist Committee on Relief works through programs that address poverty, sustainable development, global health services, and refugee and immigrant concerns. The Anglican Relief and Development Fund connects churches in challenging areas with the resources they need to effectively minister to their communities. Baptist World Aid has sought to alleviate poverty and hunger and support community development projects across the globe. Other denominations have similar programs, which when added up continue to make a significant difference in the lives of vulnerable people around the world.

---

15. Inverleigh, *Great Reformer*, 94.
16. Inverleigh, *Great Reformer*, 295.
17. Inverleigh, *Great Reformer*, 114–16.

A KINGDOM FOCUS?

Much of the political polarization in many countries is rooted in the culture wars among Christians over the issues of abortion and the rights of the LGBTQ community. Some of the conflicts have also included disputes over capitalism, illegal migration, and the role of the church in politics. Anger over these issues has split Christian traditions from one another and has even caused conflicts within denominations and congregations. Yet, as is abundantly clear, they are united in the Kingdom work of feeding the hungry, aiding the poor, providing pure water, healing the sick, providing shelter, aiding immigrants, and working for peace. Most important for the world is that Christians are also eager to speak of the work of Christ for the forgiveness of sins and the hope of the resurrection. This is the holistic view of the Kingdom, which only Christians can claim.

Why is there such polarization when Christians have so much in common? Is it because the institutions of the church have become much more important than the Kingdom of God that Jesus preached? Are the divisions rooted in the desire of the Christian communities to show that they are more right in their teachings than their opponents? Do they seek to profit from disagreements, advertising their own virtue and uniqueness? Were Christians to focus their faith and life on the promises of the Kingdom rather than on their loyalty to their church and traditions, much of the polarization would be calmed and they might see each other more clearly as fellow members of the body of Christ, united in his mission.

WORLD RELIGIONS AND HUMANISM

Christ not only works to bring more blessings of the Kingdom to our world through the efforts of Christians. He also does it through members of other religions and those who have no religion at all. In a time of religiously inspired conflicts around the world and the threat of a global conflict between civilizations rooted in religion, representatives of the world's religions, together with some humanists, gathered to see if they could forge a "Global Ethic" based on some common beliefs. This was not an attempt to create a single ideology, nor a mixture of all religions. They are so different in faith, dogma, symbols, and rites that any unification attempt would be meaningless. Nor was there an effort to replace the high ethics of individual religions with an ethical minimalism. Rather, it only sought to work out what was already common to the religions of the world and sensible ethical values held by others.[18]

Under the leadership of Roman Catholic theologian Hans Küng, in consultation with the leaders of the world's religions, a Global Ethic was produced based upon the common values of all. The Global Ethic was not written in a vacuum but was addressed to the real problems the world faced in 1993, when it was read to a plenary of the Parliament of Religion. The Declaration of the Ethic begins with the brief but devastating description of the world then and now:

> The world is in agony. The agony is so pervasive and urgent that we are compelled to name its manifestations so that the depth of this pain may be made clear. Peace eludes us . . . the planet is being destroyed . . . neighbors live in fear . . . women and men are estranged from one another . . . children die.[19]

Based on the teaching of the world's religions, they affirmed that a common set of core values form the basis of a Global Ethic. They also affirmed that there is an irrevocable, unconditional norm for all areas of life. There already exists ancient guidelines in the teachings of the world's religions for human behavior that need to be followed. The declaration asserts that "We must treat others as we wish others to treat us," thus repeating the golden rule found in all the religions. It affirms that all of humanity is our family and that we should serve others, especially children, the aged, the poor, the suffering, the disabled, the refugees, and the lonely. About war and conflict, it says that we commit ourselves to a culture of nonviolence, respect, justice, and peace. About economics, it calls for the world to move beyond the dominance of greed for power, prestige, money, and consumption to make for a more just and peaceful world.

The signatories to this global ethic include representatives of all the major religions of the world as well as many of the smaller ones. At the conclusion of the Declaration they said, "Therefore, we commit ourselves to this global ethic, to understanding one another and to socially beneficial, peace-fostering, and nature-friendly ways of life. We invite all people, religious or not, to do the same."[20] Comparing this Global Ethic with Jesus'

---

18. Küng and Kuschel, eds., *Global Ethic*, 7–8. The first meeting of the Parliament of the World's Religions was held at the Chicago World's Fair in 1893. It met again one hundred years later and has continued meeting many times since.

19. Küng and Kuschel, eds., *Global Ethic*, 13.

20. Küng and Kuschel, eds., *Global Ethic*, 14–16.

ethic of the Kingdom (Matt 25:32–46), some amazing similarities can be seen. Despite the agony of the present world, there is now a morally accepted ethic for the Kingdom of God, the New World Society.

NONGOVERNMENTAL ORGANIZATIONS

The global ethic seems almost foolishly idealistic in a world dominated by self-seeking capitalism and nation-states arming for their own security and influence. Yet a host of nongovernmental organizations (NGOs) are working diligently to live up to some of the norms of the ethic. Non-state actors are not new but have never been as large and many as they are now. Global NGOs are organizations that are not established by intergovernmental agreements. They are not for profit and cannot advocate for violence. Their main objective is to pursue political or social change without striving for government power.[21] We have already described some of the church-based NGOs. Now we will look at others coming out of civil society, foundations, and those related to the Unted Nations.

Some of the more well-known NGOs dealing with hunger, disaster relief, and development are Save the Children, the Red Cross, the Red Crescent, CARE, Mercy Corps, and Feeding America. The largest NGO in the world is the Bangladesh Rural Advancement Committee (BRAC), with 900,000 employees, 70 percent of them women. BRAC's mission is to empower people and communities in situations of poverty, illiteracy, disease, and social injustice.[22] NGOs dealing with the environment include Greenpeace, Nature Conservancy, Sierra Club, National Resource Defense, World Wildlife Fund, Flora and Fauna International, and others. Doctors without Borders, International Medical, and the Bill & Melinda Gates Foundation have been in the forefront of medical aid and disease control. Habitat for Humanity joins BRAC and other NGOs in poorer nations to build homes for people.

In the United States there are approximately 1.5 million NGOs. These include local feeding programs, dental charities, and a wide variety of organizations dealing with alcohol and drug abuse. In the general category of nongovernmental organizations are also the Ford Foundation, the Rockefeller Foundation, the Hewlett Foundation, and others. These fund a

---

21. Kaloudis, *Non-Governmental Organizations*, xvii.

22. Bangladesh Rehabilitation Assistance Committee, https://www.bracusa.org/about/.

wide variety of projects, including those that help people in need.[23] At first glance the goals of NGOs seem simple, uncomplicated, and praiseworthy. However, as NGOs seek to carry out their mission in societies dominated by conflicts, corruption, and greed, choices need to be made that dissipate the benefits of the enterprise.[24] Nevertheless, the efforts of these NGOs for the world's vulnerable and needy have been outstanding. This is especially true of NGOs connected with the United Nations.

The United Nations was created at the end of World War II. Then its chief motivation was to prevent future conflicts like two devastating wars. With respect to keeping the peace it did not live up to its founders' hope. Yet, it did end the partition of the Congo, lobbied for peace in Vietnam, supervised the end of the Iraq-Iran War, and helped end conflicts in Cyprus, Kashmir, El Salvador, Cambodia, Mozambique, Haiti, and Kosovo.[25]

NGOs connected with the UN have taken global leadership in humanitarian relief. The World Food Programme, whose director is appointed partly by the UN Secretary General, serves 160 million people in 126 countries and territories.[26] The UNHCR, the UN refugee agency, protects people forced to flee their homes due to conflict and persecution and works in more than 130 countries protecting millions of evacuees.[27] Other UN agencies that are concerned with the health and welfare of the world's sick and vulnerable are UNICEF, the Children's Fund, the World Health Organization, and UNIDO, the UN agency promoting economic development.[28]

GOD'S NEW WORLD SOCIETY IS NEAR

That sounds unbelievable as we are confronted with selfishness, greed, corruption in politics, climate change, failed states, and more war. Yet Christ is working to bring about some of the promises of his Kingdom through Christians, through people of other faiths, in NGOs, and in politics as governments help in disasters and care for the sick and starving. It is a global army of sorts, including the vast majority of the world's people who

23. Kaloudis, *Non-Governmental Organizations*, 5–12.
24. Kaloudis, *Non-Governmental Organizations*, xx.
25. Meisler, *United Nations*, 390.
26. World Food Programme, https://www.wfp.org.
27. UN High Commissioner for Refugees, https://www.unhcr.org.
28. UN Industrial Development Organization, https://www.unido.org.

are working for a better world, including the millions of ordinary people, especially the poor, who daily go out of their way to help their neighbors having a bad time. Is there a way to connect these people? This is far too vast a project for any organization. Such an institution would only create more problems. A better way to join in common tasks might be to simply follow Christ as he praised a Roman centurion for his confident faith in Christ to heal his servant (Luke 7:9). Again, he commended the Syrophoenician woman for her strong plea (Matt 15:28). What about a newsworthy article about Christians, now polarized, who would praise one another for their works of mercy? Amid an Islamic terrorist threat, what if Christians talked about BRAC, the largest NGO in the world, which has its origins in a Muslim country? Might it be possible to have a worldwide digital platform for people to share the good news of what they are doing to improve the lives of those in need? It would be another sign that God's New World Society is near.

Following Jesus' announcement of the nearness of the Kingdom, he said, "repent and believe the good news" (Mark 1:15). Like Amos, Isaiah, and Jeremiah, Jesus warned of the consequences of simply accumulating wealth. A rich man dies after achieving economic security (Luke 12:16–21). Another wealthy man ends up in torment while his poor beggar rests in Abraham's bosom (Luke 16:19–27). Commenting on a rich young man's refusal to give of his wealth to help the poor, Jesus said, "It is easier for a camel to go through the eye of a needle than for a rich man to enter the Kingdom of God" (Luke 18:22–25). What might repentance look like in "God's New World Society?" Might it look like Bob, of Bob's Red Mill, turning over his company to his faithful employees to own, manage, and prosper? What about the owner of Patagonia giving 98 percent of his company to a group fighting climate change? Could wealthy CEOs of large corporations refuse a large portion of their income so that the warehouse workers and janitors receive better wages? As inequality grows within societies and between nations, repentance can heal and even protect capitalism from its self-inflicted failure. But without the change that repentance can bring, disaster awaits.

Jesus said, "believe the good news." Faced with our current problems, that may be harder than repentance. The good news of the Kingdom is not our arrival at a plateau where all is well. Rather, as in the life of Christ, it comes through the cross, to the resurrection. As Jesus announced the good news of the Kingdom, only later to weep at the destruction of Jerusalem (Luke 19:41), so God's New World Society may grow out of the ashes of

World War III and in an almost unrecognizable world caused by climate change and human garbage. Though people from around the world are working with Christians in aiding the poor and vulnerable, in a time of disaster Christians have the special and unique insight that in Christ's suffering and death the ultimate Kingdom is already here and waiting for us in the life to come. This gives us the confidence and joy to work through the challenges we face and be hopeful in the coming and nearness of God's New World Society.

Chapter 9

Coercion vs. Consensus

GOD'S NEW WORLD SOCIETY is alive and active in works of mercy and love. It also advocates on behalf of the weak and vulnerable, hoping to influence governments to do the right thing by their own citizens and the hurting people around the world. However, as climate change accelerates, economic inequality grows, more nations arm for war, poor nations collapse, and refugees swarm to safe nations, major changes to the world system are underway. In the past there was enormous optimism about the future, but it eroded around 1968. It was an era when everyone was sure that history was on the side of progress. The state was seen as an arbitrator and mediator of reform. Now, however, there has been a loss of faith in government. At the same time, people around the world want more democracy, by which they often mean equal rights, a job and pension, good education for their children, and good medical treatment. These demands and the loss of confidence in the government will add up to more disorder and political conflict.[1] To deal with the coming strife we are confronted with a choice between states looking to more coercion through hard power, or new and better ways to build a consensus working toward the Kingdom promises. Will it come through Pilate's authority to crucify, or will it come through the soft power of another Kingdom, not from this world?

---

1. Wallerstein, *End of the World*, 17–18.

COERCION VS. CONSENSUS

AUTHORITARIAN GOVERNMENTS

Hard power is most clearly manifested in authoritarian governments. Recent political developments indicate that there is a worldwide increase in authoritarian regimes. Joining Russia and China, nations like Nicaragua and Cambodia are on the cusp of authoritarian control, as is Hungary.[2] Authoritarian governments are on the rise. Some come through coups, although these are dangerous and often fail. Others come about in democracies largely through populist appeals. A central message of populism is that the leader or leadership group alone can save the country. They claim that at this critical time, only a visionary executive can solve the nation's problems. A second message is that the current political elite are corrupt or unable to address the challenges before them. The third message is that the media and experts should not be trusted. The effort is to discredit what is accepted knowledge, especially as it has been put forth by government agencies. This is intended to weaken the ability of citizens to properly evaluate the choices they have before them.[3]

One defining feature of authoritarian rule is repression. This involves the murder of opponents or whole groups of people that challenge the government. It also jails political rivals or bans their parties from campaigning. Criticism of the government is countered by closing newspapers and imprisoning journalists. Even peaceful protests are forbidden, and activists are detained or held for years. More subtle forms of repression are surveillance of the opposition and lawsuits against opponents. Sometimes to avoid criticism, governments employ party faithful or paramilitary groups to intimidate critics of the regime. Common to most authoritarian governments is a ban on the human rights of expression, association, assembly, and beliefs.[4]

Another way authoritarian governments survive is to coopt rivals by extending benefits to potential challengers to secure their loyalty to the regime. One strategy is to grant special recognition to a variety of minority political parties to divide any major opposition. Another is to provide economic perks like paved roads or government jobs to communities that might otherwise favor the opposition. Retaining the support of the military sometimes comes by letting officers run state-owned enterprises. While

2. Frantz, *Authoritarianism*, 40.
3. Frantz, *Authoritarianism*, 99–102.
4. Frantz, *Authoritarianism*, 105–7,

neutralizing potential opposition through granting benefits is important, governments also need to be extra generous toward their most loyal supporters. Sometimes it is simple cash for support or the use of government cars. More often it is high government posts or directorship of profitable enterprises.[5] Whether they use repression or the distribution of benefits, authoritarian governments are using hard power to coerce people to do their will.

DEMOCRATIC GOVERNMENTS

Although democratic governments are not repressive in killing opponents, keeping them from running for office, or jailing reporters, they employ hard power that benefits their supporters. Even when authoritarian regimes give way and countries struggle for democratic rule, elites in the previous regime continue to have a privileged position in the new democratic government. Some who benefit from the new arrangement are those who held administrative and political positions in the old government. Other beneficiaries are wealthy landowners, manufacturers, and firms doing business with the government, whether it is authoritarian or democratic.[6] We see this pattern repeating itself, from the founding fathers in the United States to the Russian elites following the end of the Soviet Union, but there are many other examples from around the world.

Conservative politicians in democratic countries argue that in the name of stability, radical social change should be rejected. While they are not resistant to all change, they believe it should be moderated by those who know best. Not everyone in society has the knowledge and judgement to make important decisions. These should be reserved for well-known and time-honored leaders in the traditional institutions of commerce, religion, and culture. Conservatives put their faith in family, especially if the family has a hierarchical, patriarchal structure. The political strategy is clear. It is to restore and maintain traditional institutions and have the people submit to their wisdom.[7] It follows that in conservative democratic regimes, benefits and rewards go to corporations, large landowners, conservative religious groups, and their media supporters.

---

5. Frantz, *Authoritarianism*, 111–15.
6. Albertus and Menaldo, *Authoritarianism*, 31–33.
7. Wallerstein, *World Systems Analysis*, 61–62.

COERCION VS. CONSENSUS

Liberalism arose as a counter-ideology. It opposed both the reign of terror in the French Revolution and traditional hierarchies. Liberals argued that change was not only normal but could be good. They believed in a world of progress toward a better society. One aspect of the French Revolution that caught their fancy was that "careers should be open to talents." Today this sentiment would be expressed as "equal opportunity" or "meritocracy." This means that there should be a different type of hierarchy based on ability and talent. Liberalism holds that these are based upon natural hierarchies instead of inherited ones. While conservatives are the party of order, liberals are the party of progress. This means that institutions need reform. Who should take the lead in such changes? Leadership should be the province of specialists. They understand the problems and through their training are best equipped to work for a solution. This, of course, requires an education, and liberals champion specialized learning as the best preparation for those leading the nation.[8] It follows that in liberal democratic regimes the benefits and rewards go the educated, the specialists, and those whose talents have helped society move forward.

Regardless of whether liberals or conservatives are in power, there are some who are often excluded from benefits and power: common workers, racial minorities, recent immigrants, former prisoners, and the disabled. Many welcome the phrase "workers of the world unite." But would that include farmers in Ukraine? Would that include women? In America some unions resisted women workers, fearing it would lower wages. Women decided that their liberation came first. Would it include minorities? African Americans had their own struggles. Each of the excluded groups had an international side but none had the power to pursue it. Even Lenin had to decide that changes would need to be made in stages. Just organize the urban workers and then just take over one country, he advocated; others will follow. Other groups had similar strategies; women organized for suffrage and achieved it. With the civil rights movement Blacks gained the legal right to vote. In the US, the disabled achieved many of their aims. Because each group pursued its own ends, they have not been able to get together enough to become a substantial political force.[9] They have made some gains but never received the material benefits bequeathed on the conservative owners or the liberal specialists. Still excluded from even the

---

8. Wallerstein, *World Systems Analysis*, 62–63.
9. Wallerstein, *World Systems Analysis*, 67–71.

right to vote and work are the increasing number of newly arrived refugees and migrants.

Worst of all, these oppressed groups have not been able to join with their mates across the world, especially in poor nations. There, conditions for workers are deplorable even though they make goods for markets in rich nations. In traditional societies, the rights of women for education, equality, and simple human rights are almost nonexistent. Who can even list the horrors of minority groups in China, Myanmar, Iran, Afghanistan, Ethiopia, and Eritrea? Refugees camp under bridges and die crossing waters. Hard power has been hardest on those who need the most help.

HARD POWER IN INTERNATIONAL AFFAIRS

International affairs are often viewed through the lens of great power conflicts. Forgotten are the economic rivalries that caused the wars. The French and English fought over control over the money to be made in North America and India. World War I was about the German desire to rival France and England in colonial trade and possessions. Later, in World War II, Japan wished to replace America and European power in the colonization of Asia. Perhaps the chief goal in these conflicts was to profit from the underdeveloped wealth of underdeveloped countries. The Spanish stole gold; the French, furs; the English, slaves. They coveted the land for colonies, settlers, and the resultant trade that exported cheap commodities from the colonies and imported expensive manufactured goods from Europe.

Why are some nations rich and others poor? Using the nation as the unit of analysis, one theory said all nations were poor but gradually developed over time to become more prosperous. This led to the language of "developed" and "underdeveloped," or, more hopefully, "developing" nations. This concept was challenged by Raul Prebisch and other economists from Latin America. Instead of using the country as a unit of analysis, they used the whole world as a single unit. They claimed that international trade was not trade among equals, but because some nations were stronger economically, surplus wealth would flow to the stronger nations. This meant that rich nations would continue to profit from poor nations. In this world system analysis, the rich nations were referred to as the "core" and poorer nations were relegated to the "periphery."[10] When the cost of labor cuts into

---

10. Wallerstein, *World Systems Analysis*, 10–13.

profits in core nations, production is moved into some peripheral countries with lower labor costs. This process elevates these nations from the periphery to what is now termed "semi-peripheral states." These include states like South Korea, Indonesia, Brazil, India, and South Africa. While the standard of living in these nations improves for some, there are still wide swaths of poor in these societies whose lives have not changed.[11]

HARD AND SOFT POWER

Pilate's hard power could kill in the name of state security, make war, tax the public, and shower benefits on supporters, including religious leaders like those in the Sanhedrin. Hard power can also keep citizens safe, build roads, punish criminals, protect commerce, and occasionally provide welfare. With the power to coerce, it can move swiftly. Though people may not always like the hard power of governments, they do respect it and, for the most part, obey. Those exercising hard power can get things done quickly, but, ironically, they themselves do not last long. The empires in Nebuchadnezzar's dream ended routinely, one after another. Dynasties rise and fall; presidents come and go. Even great tribulations like the Babylonian captivity or communism in Eastern Europe lasted only seventy years or so.

Confronted with Pilate's power, Jesus looked helpless, a sheep ready to be slaughtered. Yet, Jesus was planting a power infinitely greater than Pilate's. It was a soft power leading to consensus. It was not possible without Jesus' death and resurrection, a once-for-all-time event. Even the crimes against humanity are forgiven and death is swallowed up so real life can be realized. Death and resurrection also set the pattern for the full exercise of soft power in the years ahead. To follow Christ in his Kingdom work, Jesus told his disciples, "If any want to become my followers, let them deny themselves and take up their cross and follow me" (Matt 16:24). Then, as Jesus said to Paul, "My grace is sufficient for you, for power is made perfect in weakness" (2 Cor 12:9).

In world politics more attention now is being given to "soft power." It rests on the ability to shape the preferences of others. One way to do this is through the power of attraction. One reason why democratic nations are more attractive to asylum seekers is because of the promises of security, freedom, and opportunity. This is also why many countries would like to be more democratic if they could. Another way in which soft power is applied

---

11. Wallerstein, *World Systems Analysis*, 28–30.

is through shared values. This explains the alliance between many English-speaking nations around the world, who were influenced by language and British democratic ideals. Soft power is also exercised through love and duty. When the United Kingdom was under attack in World War II, help came from the US, Australia, Canada, and New Zealand both because of the love and compassion they felt for the victims of the bombing and also for the duty they felt for the nation that had been so important to their existence. In these cases, soft power led to a consensus to aid the United Kingdom in its struggles.[12]

SEEKING CONSENSUS IN A DIVIDED WORLD

In *The City of God* Augustine spoke about the Kingdom and applied it to the transition coming at the end of the Roman Empire. In the transition from the church-oriented Middle Ages to the nation-state system, Luther sought to distinguish the Kingdom of God's grace from the kingdom of the state based upon law and reason. For the worldwide transition before us, can Christ's Kingdom provide a template for analysis and action? Might the soft power Christ applied at his time be the way to work in our world? In stark contrast to the polarization gripping most nations and the entire global system, Jesus' teaching can lead to consensus. In an oppressive foreign ruled country he said, "Love your enemies and pray for those who persecute you" (Matt 5:44). He reminded us that God "makes his sun rise on the evil and on the good and sends rain on the righteous and on the unrighteous" (Matt 5:45). But is consensus possible with those who kill innocent people, as happens regularly in unjust societies? To those who were nailing him to the cross, Jesus said, "Father, forgive them; for they do not know what they are doing" (Luke 23:34). Because Jesus understood his killer's ignorance, he asked that they be forgiven. Looking at the causes for the evil people do, Jesus enjoins us to see our common humanity. He challenges our judgement when he asks, "Why do you see the speck in your neighbor's eye, but do not notice the log in your own eye?" (Matt 7:3).

How can we build consensus in our contemporary world? We do it all the time as a family, but unless there is some consensus, the family will not last. Might we say the same for a society? Sometimes consensus can be achieved through an appeal to shared values. Thus, most people, most of the time, prefer prosperity to poverty, stability to conflict, and peace to

---

12. Nye, *Soft Power*, 5–8.

war. Confronted by the possibility of another world war and the challenge to all life through climate change and pollution, a consensus must and can emerge to meet these problems.[13] Consensus also can also come about when all agree to some previously agreed-upon standard such as a constitution or the UN Declaration of Human Rights.[14] Still another path to consensus is the consideration of options. This is rarely possible in democratic nations with voting for or against a candidate or proposal. It is often impossible in an authoritarian regime. Yet, it opens the possibility of compromise and greater agreement.[15]

CONSENSUS IN REPRESSIVE REGIMES

One of the greatest fears in democratic nations is that appeals to right-wing populism will lead to an authoritarian regime. This might mean loss of personal liberties, end of press freedom, persecution of minorities, and the end of religious liberty. It is estimated that 38 percent of the world's people live under authoritarian governments and 20 percent live in societies that are partially free.[16] As bad as this would be for those who have lived and fought for democracy, life goes on. Is consensus possible in situations such as these? Probably not, if by "consensus" we are speaking about a mutual exercise of government power. However, if we are speaking about learning how to live with others in an oppressive state, it has been done before and can be done in the future. When he leaders of Judah were taken into captivity in Babylon, God told them to build houses, plant gardens, marry, and pray for the welfare of their oppressors (Jer 29:4–7).

How is consensus built with others in a repressive society? Perhaps the best way is for people to work toward Kingdom goals. In Russia the tolerance of religious groups has gone back and forth from outright persecution to bureaucratic delay in granting recognition and permission to build churches. Yet one scorned Pentecostal church gained recognition and appreciation by working with addicts. Similar cases are cited in China. Because the Catholic Church recognizes only the authority of the Vatican, it is not legal in in China and has no state protection. Yet it established a presence in districts of Shanghai with little government interference.

---

13. Emerson, *Politics of Consensus*, 64–65.
14. Emerson, *Politics of Consensus*, 30–31.
15. Emerson, *Politics of Consensus*, 7–8.
16. Repucci and Slipowitz, "Global Expansion of Authoritarian Rule," 1.

This is attributed to charitable work and establishment of housing for the disabled.[17]

Not all religious groups wish to be registered with the government. Many of these are part of what has been called the "house church movement." These have taken many forms. In China, wealthy Christian businessmen have created factories with dormitories, cafeterias, bathhouses, clinics, and convenience stores. They also have Sunday services and are effective in evangelizing those who are part of their factory community. Because the factories are duly registered and are part of the planned economy model of economic production, their religious activities are known but provoke little criticism.[18] Another house church model in China is the China Gospel Fellowship. This is a group of small house churches operating in network with one to three million members. Patterned after the communist cells in Russia and China, each little church operates independently and has little or no knowledge of any other house church, so that if it is banned, the ban will not harm other churches. Though the authorities may crack down on individual house churches, the movement is so large that it is tolerated.[19] Some consensus is possible even in authoritarian nations. When Christians work toward Kingdom goals in helping the vulnerable, it even opens the door to speaking about Christ and the fuller view of the Kingdom in the forgiveness of sin and the hope of eternal life.

CONSENSUS IN DEMOCRACIES

Recently, most democracies have become deeply polarized. The recognized divisions are between the largest political parties. In the United States these are growing further apart. Pew Research Center says, "Republicans and Democrats are more divided along ideological lines—and partisan antipathy is deeper and more extensive—than at any point in the last two decades."[20] Furthermore, these parties are largely led by elites who are well educated, wealthy, and have important connections either in conservative or liberal circles. Largely unconsulted and powerless are the very poor, recent migrants, the homeless, battered women, ex-prisoners, the chronically ill, and the unemployed. These are the ones who caught Jesus' attention in

---

17. Koesel, *Religion and Authoritarianism*, 65–75.
18. Emerson, *Politics of Consensus*, 82–86.
19. Emerson, *Politics of Consensus*, 161–63.
20. Pew Research Center, "Political Polarization."

his ministry. In a democracy that is to be "of, by, and for the people," how might these have a seat at the table in making important decisions that might bring some joy their lives?

One approach might be to move away from "identity politics" to "pain politics." Now the politics in democracies that generate most passion revolve around identity. The cause may be for the women's movement, evangelical Christians, African Americans, the LGBTQ community, white nationalists, or the Chamber of Commerce. Once an identity is established, arguments are honed, enemies are labeled, and passion is unleashed. But the Kingdom route to consensus might be pain politics. What are the mothers of children slain by gun violence saying? How does it feel for an LGBTQ youth to be condemned by their parents and peers? What is the most important thing a homeless man needs first? What is it like to be hated because you are Black? It hurts to be ignored because you do not have an education. How does it feel to be despised because you are prejudiced against others?

The politics of pain can break down identities because we all have experienced it. On the deepest human level, unless our identity blocks it, we have compassion for others who are suffering. Rich people give, liberals organize, the media investigates, and Christians visit. Your political opponent is human too. That might make it easier to love him even if he does turn out to be your enemy. The politics of pain will not lead to a consensual agreement on hotly contested issues, but it can help us walk a mile in someone else's shoes to understand how others think and act. Just a little consensus can help us break through the current polarization that keeps good things from happening.

IN THE GLOBAL COMMUNITY

Consensus in the global community does happen and is expanding rapidly. International cooperation has grown quickly since World War II. Seeking to reduce tensions, promote international trade, and come together to solve problems, states have formed international organizations (IOs). It is estimated that there were 220 IOs in 1909. By 1972 there were 4,000 and currently there are more than 70,000. These are defined as bodies that promote voluntary cooperation between their members but do not have autonomous power or the authority to impose rulings on their members. These organizations include intergovernmental organizations (IGOs), which are made up of representatives of states, like the United Nations and its agencies. They also include international organizations made up of representatives of non-state actors.[21]

One of the most notable regional associations that came together after World War II was the European Coal and Steel Community (ECSC). Various proposals were made to bring Europe together after the war. Few of them had a chance to succeed given the many challenges of the time. Jean Monnet and Robert Schuman of France advanced a plan that could work.

The industrial Ruhr valley had built much of Germany's war machine. France's Alsace region had coal, but France had a smaller industrial base. This would limit France's ability to keep up with Germany should conflict break out. They saw a solution in integrating coal and steel under a new institution. It would not be "intergovernmental," limited by national concerns. Rather, it would be supranational, with the independence to bring France and Germany together in a consensual relationship.[22] While the chief motive was to bring peace between these long-time antagonists, it succeeded because it began with an economic plan that has grown to become so much more.

Building on the success of the ECSC, some proposed a European Defense Community. But several nations would not give up control of their military and the plan failed. But out of the ashes was born the conviction that it would be much better to aim for deeper economic integration. Agreement followed and in 1957 the European Economic Community (EEC) was formed.[23] The new arrangement was beneficial to Europe, and in 1990 representatives came together to form a more political entity and created the European Union (EU). However, the emphasis was not on a military hard power that would compete with the supporting nations. Rather, it was about public health, education, justice, and social policy, and it even established a common currency.[24]

Guided by the success of the European Union, other regional associations have been formed around the world. The Association of Southeast Asian Nations (ASEAN) was begun in Bangkok in 1967. In Latin America, Mercosur was created to set up a common market between Brazil, Argentina, Paraguay, Uruguay, and Venezuela, and it gave other countries associate membership. Its goal was to set up a common market like that of the

---

21. Olsen, *European Union*, 12.
22. Olsen, *European Union*, 34–35.
23. Olsen, *European Union*, 37.
24. Olsen, *European Union*, 52–53.

COERCION VS. CONSENSUS

EU. However, political issues in some of the member states have limited its progress. This has also been the experience of the Pan-Africanism movement in Africa.

Kwame Nkrumah of Ghana proposed an Organization of African Unity (OAU). Founded in 1963, the organization's first proposal was to unify the independent states of Africa. However, this political objective was opposed by some of the larger states. It subsequently concentrated on the elimination of colonialism and racial rule on the continent. With the freedom of Namibia and the end of Apartheid in South Africa, it achieved some of its goals. However, it failed to meet the expectations of the people for a united and prosperous future.[25] To address the pressing everyday needs of Africans, a successor organization was set up in 2002 called the African Union (AU). Its primary purpose was to concentrate on sustainable development, good governance, and the economic well-being of the population.[26]

Consensus is possible. It takes place in repressive and democratic regimes. Even nations of the world come together for their mutual advantage. However, if we are at the beginning of a historical system shift with all its uncertainty and dangers, will consensus work? Looking ahead, Wallerstein speculates, "In constructing the successor system (or systems) to our existing one, we shall be opting either for a hierarchical system, bestowing or permitting privileges according to rank in the system, however this rank is determined (including meritocratic criteria), or for a relatively democratic, relatively egalitarian system."[27]

Jesus gathered people together announcing the coming of the Kingdom and doing Kingdom stuff like feeding, healing, forgiving, and raising the dead. In the challenging days ahead, the temptation will be to control the chaos through hard power. Yet Jesus' way is to mercifully help, persevere through hard times, and over the centuries inspire the consensus that can lead to hope and survival.

---

25. Mathews, "African Union," 18.
26. Rukato, "African Union," 110.
27. Wallerstein, *World System Analysis*, 89.

Chapter 10

Amazement and Energizing

How is it that people can remain so calm in the face of the coming disasters caused by human greed? The planet burns, floods, and turns fields into deserts. Billions spent on weapons can't be spent on schools, clinics, and aid to refugees. The weapons are meant to prepare to keep the peace, but they instead provide the path to war. Yet in the face of these disasters, vacations are still taken, homes are bought and sold, and people get married and watch football.

Walter Brueggemann, a student of the Old Testament prophets, describes the calmness of people in the face of catastrophe as a *"numbness."* He claims that this does not just happen. Rather, it is intentionally planned by people in power. He examines the court of Solomon and the kings who followed. Their power rested on three pillars. One, they were supported by the affluent, who benefitted from their rule. Two, the lifestyles of these rich depended upon the exploitation of the poor. Three, the whole system rested on a religion that was a cheerleader for the state. God was safely housed in the temple and honored for the sake of the system. It was truly a "royal consciousness." All rested on the stability of the scheme; all produced the *"numbness."*[1] Today, we might call it the powerlessness of the people.

CONTEMPORARY NUMBNESS

On the international level, the power in control is the system of capitalism and its symbiotic relationship with nation-states. Even though there are

---

1. Brueggemann, *Prophetic Imagination*, 26–31.

several communist nations that do not consider themselves capitalist, they are still subject to the system that controls investment, intellectual property, raw materials, and foodstuffs. Like the kings of old, the current system also rests on the three pillars of support by the rich, neglect—if not oppression—of the poor, and the pseudo-religious belief in capitalism itself. Producing almost unimaginable wealth for many for the past five hundred years, its powerful defenders have an almost sacred devotion to its relevance and worth. When communism proved a poor adversary, capitalism remains as a "royal consciousness," governing the way that people act and think. It also has created that vast "*numbness*" that keeps us calm with tragedies going on all around us. We are reminded that there is little we can do to change the way things are.

Even if we could do something, what would we do? Intellectually we have come to an impasse caused by the division between the humanities, with their ethics, and the social sciences, which have limited themselves to study what is rather than what should be. Economics charts the differences between rich and poor but rarely takes strong positions on how to address the issues. Political science describes how the system works but is not expected to take sides on how to change it. In the problem of failed states and homeless refugees, social science analyzes the problems, but without clear remedies the analyses are next to useless. As a result, social science is in the process of staying outside of the struggle to achieve human freedom and collective welfare.[2] With the separation of morality from the scientific tools to make a difference, the *numbness* just gets worse.

THE GIFT OF TEARS

The crying of a baby gets our attention. We are awakened from sleep. In the Old Testament Jeremiah breaks through the *numbness* with an anguished cry as he contemplates the end of the nation. "My anguish, my anguish! I writhe in pain! Oh, the walls of my heart! My heart is beating wildly; I cannot keep silent; for I hear the sound of the trumpet, the alarm of war. Disaster overtakes disaster, the whole land is laid waste" (Jer 4:19–20). With poetry the prophet invades the comfort of the people. Here there is no political opposition, no alternative party platform. Here is just the revelation that it will all be gone—government, temple, culture, and for many, life itself.

2. Wallerstein, *End of the World*, 154–56.

Like Jeremiah, Jesus cried. Looking at Jerusalem, he said, "Indeed, the days will come upon you, when your enemies will set up ramparts around you and surround you and hem you in on every side. They will crush you to the ground, you and your children within you, and they will not leave within you one stone upon another, because you did not recognize the time of your visitation from God" (Luke 19:43–44). Commenting on the power of grief as a wake-up call, Brueggemann writes that grief and mourning, crying in public, is the ultimate jarring criticism of the *numbness* we feel when confronted by the injustices all around us.[3]

Today we are reminded of the death of our climate by the children leaving school in protest against all of us unthinkingly warming it up. Inspired by Greta Thunberg, an environmental activist, more than a million young people in 2,083 cities in 175 countries raised awareness of the destructiveness of climate change. One of their signs said, "You say you love your children, but you are destroying their future."[4] We are also reminded of the death of our young people due to gun violence. More than 370,000 students have experienced gun violence at school since Columbine. There were more school shootings in 2022—forty-six—than in any year since at least 1999.[5] Beyond the dead and wounded, children who witnessed the violence or cower behind locked doors to hide from it, can be highly traumatized. In Afghanistan, women are denied education, freedom, careers, and hope for a better life. It is reported that one or two Afghan women commit suicide every day.[6] The death of our climate, our children, mothers, and the hungry pierces our consciousness. If it causes us to pause and reconsider, it may be a gift of tears.

FIFTY YEARS LEFT?

While those deaths disturb, they are, for the most part, happening to someone else. Looming in the future is the loss of our own income and the end of our safety. Immanuel Wallerstein observes that we are now in a transformational period in the entire world system. The nation-state system and the capitalism that has fueled it for the last five hundred years is under severe threats. The first is the shortage of low-cost labor. This is the result of the

---

3. Brueggemann, *Prophetic Imagination*, 46.
4. Iberdrola, "Young People Rise Up."
5. Cox et al., "More than 370,000 Students."
6. UN News, "In Afghanistan, Women Take Their Lives."

deruralization of the world. What previously was an inexhaustible supply of people coming off the farm and willing to work for low wages is coming to an end. In the industrial world there are simply not enough people to accept the pay for working in rest homes, fast food restaurants, childcare, and entry-level in factories across the globe. This shortage results in attracting more migrants looking for work. When they are turned back at the borders, employers need to raise wages that cut deeply into their profits.

A second threat is the escalating cost of paying for climate change. In the past firms were able to discharge, pollute, exhaust, extract, mine, and poison without being charged for it. Society at large was expected to provide remedies for these problems, thus relieving the companies from having to pay for these costs of production. As long as these costs were low, not much attention was paid to them. Suddenly the world is concerned with ecology and the costs incurred by enterprises is enormous. If they are required to pay the costs of pollution, emissions, and environmental degradation, their profit margins will catapult downward. Even if they avoid direct responsibility, the public will tax them to address the damage.

A third trend limiting capital accumulation is the worldwide desire for a better life. No longer content with poverty and hopelessness, people across boundaries are demanding jobs, education, medical care, and housing. All of these are expensive and take a major bite out of the total of the world's surplus value or profits. Now states wrestle whether these costs should be paid into social welfare programs to meet these demands or whether the funds will be paid into the military to quell disorder when the demands are not met.[7] When poor nations struggle with these issues, is it any wonder why corporations hesitate to invest in them even with their cheaper labor?

Together with the failure of capitalism is the decline of state structures everywhere. This is most evident in the poorer nations but will also affect core countries. What will happen to the security of the structures as governments weaken? We may be seeing the demise of a whole historical system with all of the uncertainty and struggles that will bring. How long do we have? Wallerstein says, "We can assert that it is unlikely that the present historical system will last too much longer (perhaps fifty years at most)."[8] Will that modern prophecy also help overcome the *numbness*? We do not know what type of system or structure will replace it. While the probability of this change is frightening, it is also a creative moment. If the

---

7. Wallerstein, *End of the World*, 130–31.
8. Wallerstein, *End of the World*, 132.

present structures with their successes and injustices give way, what can we do now to prepare for a freer and fairer world?

PROPHETIC AMAZEMENT

What can you say when the end of everything you know and count on is going to end? A serious discussion of alternatives is not going to do it. Organization and protests have their place, but if the government you seek to change will simply cease to exist, what is the use? The prophets addressed the *numbness* not only by announcing impending doom but also by poetically painting amazing symbols of hope. Not just pipe dreams, these symbols reflected what God had done before and can do again. Like ripened fruit in a tree that is about to be cut down, Isaiah sings of a feast of food and wine, so much better than the manna God had provided before (Isa 25:6). More impressive than water coming out of a rock in Exodus was the promise that waters will break forth in the wilderness and streams in the desert (Isa 35:6). Before God had healed the serpent's bite; now he will make the blind see, the deaf to hear, and the lame to leap (Isa 35:5–6).

In captivity, that interminable time of loss, forgiveness was key. Second Isaiah amazes the captives when he sings, "Comfort, O comfort my people, says your God. Speak tenderly to Jerusalem, and cry to her that she has served her term, that her penalty is paid, that she has received from the LORD's hand double for all her sins" (Isa 40:1–2). The "amazement" the prophet brings to a people who lost their government is that God is now King. Jerusalem, with its burnt temple and broken walls, will be the center of a new Kingdom. The poetry glows: "Get you up to a high mountain, O Zion, herald of good tidings; lift up your voice with strength, O Jerusalem, herald of good tidings, lift it up, do not fear; say to the cities of Judah, 'Here is your God!' See, the Lord GOD comes with might, and his arm rules for him; his reward is with him, and his recompense before him" (Isa 40:9–10). But what a King he is: "He will feed his flock like a shepherd; he will gather the lambs in his arms, and carry them in his bosom, and gently lead the mother sheep" (Isa 40:11). For such a King, it is song time. *Numbness* has been invaded by the threat of extinction and now by the joy of a King's largesse. King of Jerusalem, God is a warrior to help, with the compassion of a shepherd to care.[9]

---

9. Brueggemann, *Prophetic Imagination*, 69–74.

Amazement and Energizing

CONTEMPORARY AMAZEMENT

The secularization of society has been a continuing feature of the modern world system. Where theology was once held as dominant way of knowing, this was rejected and replaced by philosophy. Later this too was challenged by critics who insisted on the necessity of evidence based upon another form of knowledge they called "science." Science has been invaluable in producing the fruits of the Kingdom in food production, medical breakthroughs, and the blessings of modern life. However, in controverted issues, limiting themselves to what was observable and measurable, scientists did not feel that they had the tools to discern what was good or bad. They left those issues to be decided by theologians or philosophers.[10] Should scientists build a nuclear bomb? Science discovered that this was possible. Politicians said that it should be done. But was it good for humanity to do so? The divorce between the two ways of knowing has been problematic and in the case of Hiroshima and Nagasaki, tragic.

In contemporary society, questions of good and evil, whatever their source, have become politicized. Positions are taken that often reflect the self-interest of the groups that advocate them. Needless to say, this leads to the polarization of whole populations and grinding inaction to address critical life-and-death issues. Is there a way to move beyond polarization? Is there anything like a contemporary "amazement" that will provide the energy to give birth to a new reality?

Wallerstein proposes that we end the divorce between the search for truth and the search for goodness. He states that "the possible is richer than the real." What we understand as real has actually been constructed from an enormous complexity of things and has been given order by people who benefit most from it. But there are other "possibilities" that may be richer and better than the order we see and one that may soon pass away. If so, we should be discussing analyzing the possible and exploring the possible. We might call this "utopistics." Wallerstein defines the term: "Utopistics is the analysis of possible utopias, their limitations and constraints in achieving them. It is the analytic study of real historical alternatives in the present. It is the reconciliation of the search for truth and the search for goodness."[11] If the next twenty-five to fifty years will be bad in human social relationships, they may also be exciting in the field of knowledge. Breakthroughs in

---

10. Wallerstein, *End of the World*, 186–87.
11. Wallerstein, *End of the World*, 217.

the fields of human welfare in the past can be mined for utopistics for the future. The possible will be richer than the real.[12]

FORGIVENESS AND RECONCILIATION

The hatred and conflicts we see all around us will come to an end as people forgive one another and are reconciled. We know about the catastrophe of war and the hatred of those of a different race. Political polarizations make good governance difficult if not impossible. Yet only forgiveness makes social life possible. It is key to marriage, child rearing, and the workplace. Forgiveness is the very foundation of the Jewish religion and the Christian faith. It allows us to lead wholesome, happy lives, freed from guilt. Though forgiveness and reconciliation seem impossible in society, politics, and international relations, it is happening. South Africa, after ending Apartheid, established the Truth and Reconciliation Commission, which eased tensions between the Black and white communities.[13] This commission, together with Nelson Mandela's own commitment to forgive, provided inspired the South African government to take a leadership role in all of Africa for human rights, democracy, and good governance.[14] Praying for the Kingdom, we add, "And forgive us our trespasses as we forgive those who trespass against us."

CASHLESS HEALING

When a young doctor was asked what her "impossible" dream of the best medical system was, she said, "cashless medicine." Jesus never charged for healing. Soldiers, wounded in combat, receive free medical care. On occasion physicians and dentists visit poor neighborhoods and do what they can to bring a little bit of healing to those who need it most. Under some national healthcare systems there are attempts to provide free medical aid. Yet, objections are made that waiting times for care are too long; there are not enough doctors or space in hospitals. Might the "impossible" dream be augmented with free medical school? If the higher income that physicians now receive was limited, would anyone want study that hard and long to be

---

12. Wallerstein, *End of the World*, 218–19.
13. Welsh, *Rise and Fall of Apartheid*, 570.
14. Landsberg, "Caught between Pan African Solidarism," 236.

a physician? Yet, around the world there are physicians, poorly paid, who are motivated by the good they can do to help their patients.

Medical problems are magnified in those nations that are experiencing disasters or conflicts. Some help comes through nongovernmental organizations like Doctors without Borders. Other notable efforts have been made by Cuba, a socialist country, which provides free healthcare to all its citizens. It also provides free medical education to thousands of students. Even though its facilities are limited by US sanctions, it provides a lot of care with very few resources. As such it is a model for many other poorer countries who have requested Cuban doctors to help them in their time of need.[15]

WORKER OWNED ENTERPRISES

The days are coming when corporations will be owned by their workers. Might this be a fulfillment of the prophecy that everyone will sit under their own vine and fig tree (Mic 4:4)?

Much of the inequality in the world is caused by executives and boards of corporations, virtually setting their own compensation based upon how much they have earned for their investors. Much of that surplus income comes from the wages of the workers. Were workers the owners, they could help set the rewards of both management and labor as well as building loyalty to the firm and working hard to produce products and provide services.

In the United States there are already more than six thousand companies where workers own some shares of their companies.[16] Not all of these firms are employee controlled. In addition, those that are 100-percent employee owned may find it difficult to compete for investment funds and other benefits in a marketplace geared for investor-owned corporations. Nevertheless, they have been very successful with rapid growth and employee satisfaction.[17] However, some of the most egregious inequality of the world is found in nations where corporations exploit the resources of poor nations in drilling for oil and mining gold, diamonds, and minerals. What would the employee ownership of such companies look like?

---

15. Conversion, "Is the Cuban Healthcare?"
16. United States Chamber of Commerce, "What Is an Employee Owned Company?"
17. Rosen and Querry, "How Well Is Employee Ownership Working?"

FOOD FOR ALL

The prophets said that there will be food for everyone, good food, and plenty of it. Given the present reality, this is truly unbelievable. Depriving the enemy of food has always been a weapon of war. In the destruction of Jerusalem, the people were so hungry that "The hands of compassionate women have boiled their own children; they became their food in the destruction of my people" (Lam 4:10). Yet, to those about to face such carnage Isaiah promised, "On this mountain the LORD of hosts will make for all peoples a feast of rich food, a feast of well-aged wines, of rich food filled with marrow, of well-aged wines strained clear" (Isa 25:6). What an amazing promise, and applied to those in conflict areas and others suffering from floods and droughts, how unbelievable! In the contrast between those suffering from obesity and others of starvation, food for all would truly be amazing.

It is estimated that between 720 and 811 million people in the world faced hunger in 2020; by 2030 it is expected that 660 million will still be hungry.[18] Looking ahead to the disasters caused by global warming, a major war, and the transition from the present world system to something else, it is expected that hunger will only increase. Through a wide variety of food programs, a beginning is being made to give minimum help to those suffering from famine. Yet, provision for eliminating hunger in the midst of worldwide crises is still in the realm of utopistics; an amazing and invigorating hope.

WATER

According to the prophets, it will come to pass that there will be enough water for irrigation, for cities, for bathing, cleaning, drinking, and animals. It will be pure water and so close to home that children can go to school instead of carrying water. Does not God pour it out of a rock? And God promises, "I will open rivers on the bare heights, and fountains in the midst of the valleys; I will make the wilderness a pool of water, and the dry land springs of water" (Isa 41:18). This sounds like foolishness, sheer foolishness, when nations may soon go to war over water. Crises over a proposed Ethiopian dam, disputes between China and India, famine in Afghanistan,

---

18. United Nations, "Food."

and the Israeli/Palestine conflict revolve around water. It is clear competition for water will escalate as climate change restricts access to water.[19]

Prophetic amazement rested on what God had done in the past. Utopistics is about possible utopias, their limitations, and overcoming the restraints to achieve them. There is no shortage of water on the earth. Technologies also exist to conserve, purify, store, and transport it to where it is most needed. While war may be contemplated to fight over this precious, limited resource, a better way to spend the money might be to increase the supply of drinkable water.

CITIES OF REFUGE

To equip refugees for their new lives and to help minor criminals to reenter society, we will have cities of refuge. The very existence of the Jewish identity comes from their liberation from a nation that was killing their children and stealing their labor. Refugees are flooding the world for some of the same reasons. They come for their children and for a place where they can be secure and find work that rewards their labor. At the same time thieves, drunk drivers, and those who have committed manslaughter need a place where they live safely, earn a living to pay for their crimes, reenter society, and learn how to govern themselves.

No nation is handling the refugee and migrant crisis well. Nor is it good to incarcerate minor offenders alongside hardened criminals. The covenant law created cities of refuge for those who killed accidentally without intent (Num 35:11–15). There they would be safe and could earn a living. Such cities of refuge could also provide a coordinated approach to supplying refugees and immigrants their basic needs. These needs are assistance in healthy nutrition, food, shelter, energy, education, and job training.[20] In the Bible these cities were spread quite evenly across the land. This might be a pattern worth copying in the crisis now occurring the major cities of the world.

---

19. Carnegie Endowment for International Peace, "Water Way."
20. UNHCR, "Basic Needs Approach."

PEACE BETWEEN NATIONS

The day is coming when all people on earth will share a common citizenship. This will make war unnecessary. "They shall beat their swords into plowshares, and their spears into pruning hooks; nation shall not lift up sword against nation, neither shall they learn war anymore" (Isa 2:4). People will be free to work and travel wherever they are needed. No longer will some be stopped at borders or treated as "second class citizens." All will be equal with common rights, benefits, and responsibilities.

Though this seems impossible and totally unreal in our divided world, its basis is the creation of all humanity by God. Historically we know that after calamity comes consensus. In everyday life we see what happens after a tornado rips apart a town. Citizens come together to help, to share, to pray. Differences are forgotten as survival becomes more important. This is true even on the global scene. After World War I much of the world came together to form the League of Nations; it was imperfect, but still significant. After World War II, we created the United Nations. Both were unthinkable in the so-called real world of 1900. Yet they happened. Will "world citizenship" take place after World War III? Might this qualify as utopistic? Might this be included when we pray, "Thy Kingdom come?"

As amazing as these images are, our hopes are quickly dashed as we are overwhelmed by the greed and selfishness of sinful people. In this world Jesus said we would have wars and rumors of wars in the end times, not peace and prosperity. Yet in the promises of the Kingdom, the New World Society, sin and evil are not the final answer. Christ has won the battle, and he will get us through death and destruction, both now and forever.

Chapter 11

The Church in Exile

IF OUR PRESENT WORLD SYSTEM has only fifty more years before it transitions into something else, what will happen to the church as we know it? In Europe and America, the institutional church has already begun to erode as millions have left. Perhaps in time of crisis, some will return, but others will continue in exile from the organized churches. Some church buildings will be sold; others will take all their members' energy and resources to keep the church repaired and doors open. For the young people who have left, where will they find the hope, focus, inspiration, and endurance to meet the struggles ahead?

When Jerusalem was destroyed and the Jewish leaders were taken in exile, the threat to the faith was real. Nothing was ever heard from the elite of the ten tribes of Israel after they had been taken into Assyria. Would that now happen to Judah? With the temple destroyed, the priests scattered, and the nation dissolved, might the faith disappear? It did not. The captives got together, studied the Word, and encouraged one another in their loss. From these humble meetings emerged what was to become the Jewish synagogue.

Another exile occurred when the disciples and Paul left the temple and the religious establishment in Jerusalem. In the wider world there were still the synagogues, but they proved hostile to the Christian message. In that exile disciples gathered in houses or wherever to share the good news and encourage one another in their faith (Acts 12:12). In exile, old patterns of living and worshipping are broken. Out of grim necessity new solutions to old patterns need to be found. While this produces anxiety for some, it can bring creativity and excitement to others.

FORGIVENESS AND RECONCILIATION

"Though your sins are like scarlet, they will be like snow" (Isa 1:18). It is a common enough message in church and taken for granted in permissive societies. In secular circles sin is seldom mentioned, yet all are aware of the problems caused by human selfishness. Part of the apathy in talking about sin is that it is often used by religious folk simply to condemn the behavior of others. Whether loudly proclaimed or seldom mentioned, sin can separate people from God and from each other. What happens when people who were raised in the church and stopped going, for whatever reason? In the introduction, we met Pastor Mike's daughter, Jane, who left the church because she was more interested in working for climate change. Staring at her cell phone, Jane cannot believe the vitriol heaped on her by one whom she thought was a good friend. Called lazy and insensitive with regard to their climate change project, the accusation really hurt, in part because it had in it elements of truth. Would their group fall apart? What a mess!

In the days to come there still will be forgiveness from Christ, guiltless confidence, reconciliation of polarized people, and a joyous hope for the future. And all this will come when churches are being sold. Like the other promises of the prophets, this one too is utopistic. That means that there is evidence that historically this can work. In Babylon there was the primitive synagogue, in which there was the hope of forgiveness even without the sacrifices in the temple. In the Roman Empire there was the house church, where forgiveness in Christ was shared in words and in communion with God and each other. Now when church buildings are being converted into restaurants and theaters, there can and will be other forms of the church.

THE END OF DEATH

Isaiah promised, "And he will destroy on this mountain the shroud that is cast over all peoples, the sheet that is spread over all nations; he will swallow up death forever" (Isa 25:7–8). Then Jesus said, "I am the resurrection and the life. Those who believe in me, even though they die, will live, and everyone who lives and believes in me will never die" (John 11:25–26). In the introduction we also met Pastor Kansa's son, Haro, who left the church in Ethiopia and went to Europe to find a better life. These words of resurrection ring in Haro's ears as he gets on the creaky boat destined for Europe. They give him courage even though he knows that many migrants from Africa never make it. Should he share his hope with others on the overcrowded deck?

The days are coming that people will talk together about death and resurrection with new urgency. Aftershocks frighten the few left alive after thousands perished. Floods wash away lives; mudslides bury families. Huddled in trenches, soldiers fear the next barrage. Then, in a beautiful retirement center another person is missing. Will I be next? What is it like to die? Can we talk about it? Jesus said, "For where two or three are gathered in my name, I am there among them" (Matt 18:20). Then Paul proclaims, "When this perishable body puts on imperishability, and this mortal body puts on immortality, then the saying that is written will be fulfilled: 'Death has been swallowed up in victory'" (1 Cor 15:54).

THE KINGDOM CHURCH

The pattern of the church in the book of Acts suggests that good news of the Kingdom is more important than the present institutional framework of the church. The real good news is that God is King here on earth, bringing forgiveness, food, healing, liberation, jobs, homes, peace between peoples and the resurrection of the dead. For many in the church the realization of God's Kingdom can come when we confess those sins of diverting resources into the church instead of for the world and believing the good news that the promises of the Kingdom can come to pass (Mark 1:15).

Nowhere will the good news of the Kingdom be more welcomed than in camps of refugees. While some live in tented camps bored with endless waiting, others shelter from the rain under bridges or risk their lives at sea. While the world turns its face away with embarrassment, some from the church bring food and shelter. Doctors and nurses volunteer in dangerous places. But who will bring the good news of forgiveness, love for one's enemies, baptism, and communion with Christ in such strange and hostile settings? When the energies of the churches are spent in keeping the institution alive, and mission dollars are spent to plant self-supporting congregations, little is left for those fleeing danger or despair. In the book of Acts, prompted by the vision of Christ and the Kingdom, the church responded to crises in wondrous ways. Can the contemporary church do the same?

OPEN DOOR TO MINISTRY

In the early church how did so few people accomplish so much?[1] They were taught by Christ, inspired by the Spirit, and gifted in some amazing ways. That's all true. But there is also a glaring difference between Act's Kingdom church and ours. It is the definition of "the ministry" and the theological education for it. In most contemporary churches, "the ministry" refers to men and women who have received their theological education in a university or seminary, devote their full-time to ministerial tasks, and are usually professionally paid for their service. All of this requires money to educate, house, and support those who publicly preach, baptize, and preside at the Lord's Supper. Then, when money is not available, ministry is limited or just does not happen.

Contrast that with the ministry in the book of Acts. Instead of a ministry concentrated in a profession, it was shared by the apostles, prophets, teachers, deacons, and elders, who were sometimes called "overseers" or "bishops." At times, these church workers received donations, and at other times, like Paul, they worked at another vocation (Acts 18:3). Churches could be planted everywhere, whether people were rich or poor, because the ministry was conducted by elders from within the new gathering (Acts 14:23). They encouraged one another with the basic gospel they had heard and celebrated Communion with the simple words of institution. If the congregation was large, they could rent a hall (Acts 19:9). If there were very few, they could still be a church.

Theological education took place in the crucible of ministry rather than in a classroom. The leaders of the new congregations faced doctrinal divides, ethical issues, and false teachers. These were addressed by letters from Paul, James, Peter, and John. Teachers like Timothy, Titus, Apollos, Jude, Priscilla, and Aquila strengthened the ministries. Seminars led by Paul provided continuing education (19:9). When the troubling argument about gentiles keeping the law came up, Paul and Barnabas went to Jerusalem to consult with James and the other leaders there, and then passed down the compromise to the churches (15:21–29).

---

1. Roland Allen, addressing missionary practices of the modern church, attributes the rapid growth of the church in the first centuries to what he called "spontaneous expansion." Allen, *Spontaneous Expansion*, 6–7.

RESHAPING THE MINISTRY

In the West, as congregations dwindle and pastors fear for their salaries, the model of ministry in Acts might provide a ray of hope. No congregation is too small to be the church in all its fullness. Elders can be recognized and equipped for essential ministry functions. If congregants are hesitant in one town, are there some in a neighboring town who would love to serve? If the seminary-educated pastor no longer can be paid, might the sale of the church help him or her serve or begin other congregations? Alternatively, the pastor could take other work, like helping settle refugees in town or running for mayor.

In the Global South, and in many poor countries, the Christian church is expanding rapidly. People flock to churches, which are often seen as a hope for a better life in this world and the next. However, it is often difficult to adequately minister to people in hard-to-reach places. Small communities in remote areas do without the sacraments for months. Because of the lack of more seminary-trained missionaries and the funds to pay them, the growth of the church is also hindered in confrontation with communities with a different culture, even within the same nation. These are also situations in which a different definition of ministry and a different approach to theological education might help.

What happens when congregations are so bound to their own traditions and culture that they are unable to see the mission to contemporary "gentiles" all around them? Might this be the time to start over and spread the good news of the Kingdom to those who like Jesus but have had problems with the organized church? Is there mission money for this? If not, might new Pauline missionaries do some self-supporting work? With a reshaped ministry, no funds would be required to buy property, pay for seminary training, or pay professional salaries. From a simple Bible class or discussion group, can a small church be started? From that group leaders can emerge and be blessed to baptize, share the Lord's Supper, and help to realize Kingdom among us.

TEACHING AND DOCTRINE

If ordinary church members with just a minimum of theological education are given responsibility for leading a small church, what will happen to the doctrine of the church? Will these leaders be capable of teaching their fellow members? Given the overwhelming secularism of the age, or the challenge of world religions on their doorstep, will not their little churches simply disappear? Roland Allen, a missionary to China in the late nineteenth century, advocated doing mission work like St. Paul did, placing the nurturing and leadership of the small churches in the hands of elders coming from those communities. When challenged that this would undermine the doctrine and teaching of the church, Allen wrote, "Paul seems to have left his newly founded churches with a simple system of Gospel teaching, two sacraments, a tradition of the main facts of the death and resurrection, and the Old Testament."[2]

Allen argued that the small content of teaching the elders had received was not an argument against ordaining them for ministry but for it. It enabled the simple message to be easily passed on and absorbed. It also left the young churches one of the most instructive aspects of their faith—their liberty. They had the freedom to grow and to fail. When challenged that Paul's practice was responsible for the Galatians losing the gospel, Allen replied that Paul never apologized for entrusting the elders with the ministry, and that he insisted that the churches there should preserve and sustain their freedom.[3]

THE CULTURAL DIMENSION

Christian leaders who have had the greatest appreciation of the biblical pattern of ministry have been those ministering to people of widely different cultures. In Tanzania, Vincent Donovan, a Roman Catholic priest, helped the Masai people come to their own understanding of baptism and the Eucharist.[4] For Donovan the best candidates for the priesthood were an elder who was illiterate, a woman who could explain the Christian message to non-Christians, one who was a good prayer, and another who preached good sermons. In that place, together, they would continue the ministry of the church.[5]

In India, Dayanand Bharati, a serious student of Allen and the biblical pattern of ministry, is a leader among a group of Christ Bhaktas. These are upper-caste Hindus who are reluctant to give up their Hindu culture, but

2. Allen, *Missionary Methods*, 116.
3. Allen, *Missionary Methods*, 119.
4. Schmidt, "Ministry of Expansion," in Allen, *Ministry of Expansion*, 35–38.
5. Donovan, *Christianity Rediscovered*, 116.

who have come to faith in Jesus through visions, healings, and answers to prayers. While many of the lower-caste Dalits (previous called "untouchables") joined Christian missionary churches, the upper-caste Hindus are reluctant to do so. For these believers, baptism is a family rite and communion is called *prasad*, an Indian word meaning "grace." Since all of this is done in a home or a small gathering, the leadership naturally arises from within the group.[6]

The United States is currently experiencing what is being called a "culture war" that pits conservatives against progressives. While conservatives often have some roots in evangelical and traditional Roman Catholic churches, many in the progressive or "liberal" culture have left the churches. *Christianity Today* reports, "Young people, those who are single, and self-identified liberals ceased attending religious services at all at much higher rates than other Americans."[7] With the promises of the Kingdom as the very heart of the Christian faith, is this a time when that message might be communicated through small group gatherings on the model of the New Testament house churches? Much will depend on what might be called the "evangelism of the Kingdom," discussed in the next chapter.

COMMUNION

One difference between a small group operating out of a local congregation and a house church is that the latter is a complete church with baptism and the Lord's Supper. Allen had no doubt that all the house churches in the New Testament habitually gathered around "the Table of the Lord."[8] Following the example of Christ when he broke the bread and shared the wine, the chief qualification of those who would do so again was to be one who serves. Right after the First Supper, the disciples debated on who would be the greatest in the Kingdom. Jesus identified himself, the presider, as one who serves (Luke 22:24–27). In the long history of the church, the Lord's Supper has divided Christians, has been weaponized against the opponents of church leaders, and has made the professionalization of the clergy, their education, and their financial support necessary. It was not so in the beginning.

---

6. Bharati, *Living Water in Hindu Bowl*, 88.
7. Roach, "Church Attendance Dropped."
8. Allen, *Missionary Methods*, 116.

There was a problem with celebrating the Lord's Table in Corinth, but it was not the qualification of the presider. Instead, it was a failure to honestly break down the differences between Christians. The slaves who cleaned the house and prepared the meals were shut out of the Communion. Here one wryly remembers Jesus' story of a banquet where they went out into the highways and byways to bring in the homeless for a meal (Luke 14:23). Then there were also the pseudo-theological divisions among the Corinthian church members. In their communion with the Lord at the Table, they had failed to discern the body of Christ among themselves (1 Cor 11:17–33). Jesus had served bread and wine, his body and blood, in a "Kingdom meal." He would not eat it again until it is fulfilled in the Kingdom of God (Luke 22:16). This means that our Lord's Suppers are "Kingdom suppers," not perfect, but just a foretaste, an appetizer, of the Kingdom feast to come.

HOUSE CHURCHES

All around the world Christians are gathering in house churches. Long an advocate and recorder of this form of the church, Wolfgang Simson writes, "In total there are currently (mid 2021) at least 22.6 million house churches world-wide with a total of around 300 million members."[9] One thousand new house churches have been started in Germany. Most of them there are made up of people who have never been Christian before. A good number are people from what was formerly East Germany, which was officially atheistic.[10] In China, where Roland Allen served as a missionary and began to advocate lay-led churches that would enable small groups of Christians to be fully the church, there are an estimated ten million house churches. It is also estimated that there are two million in India, Egypt, and the rest of the Middle East.[11]

Champions of the house church are quick to point out their New Testament roots and extensive growth, especially in lands where the Christian faith has been repressed, if not persecuted. However, there is little data on beliefs and the life of such groups. While there was a lot of enthusiasm for house churches in America as the millennial generation started leaving the

---

9. Simson, "House Church Global Report."
10. Christian Network Europe, "Secret Behind 1,000 New House Churches."
11. "House Church."

organized church around 2006,[12] that seems less true in 2023. The purposes of the house churches varies from spiritual growth to evangelism to dealing with personal problems. Some have connections with organized congregations, while others are incorporated into house church networks.

Will house churches, led by Allen's "volunteer clergy," be the vehicle for working for Christ on Kingdom promises? Much will depend upon the resilience of churches in North America. It also will hinge on how all institutions grapple with the challenges of climate change, economic disruption, and the potential of war. Most important will be the role of a modern equivalent of St. Paul. He began some churches spelling out the good news of Christ crucified, healing some, and collecting money for the poor. Other churches, like the one in Colossae, were started by others. However, in all cases, Paul continued the instruction and applied the good news to the situations in which they found themselves. From that solid foundation the churches grew and spread throughout the Roman Empire.

CHRIST'S MESSENGERS

The ordination or blessing of lay people to lead churches and celebrate the sacraments almost seems anti-intellectual. Yet, that is balanced by the education, experience, and dramatic call of St. Paul. It may be time for seminaries, now struggling to produce enough pastors for dwindling congregations, to prepare some to serve or start small churches and be theologically equipped to train the laity for their ministry. Then Bible classes might include exegesis leading to sermon preparation or intense Bible discussions. A study on Communion might lead to how to celebrate it in a rest home or a university dorm. Not only would lay people learn about baptism, but they would be taught how to instruct a person in the faith before they baptized them. An even more daunting challenge will be to seek to connect the small churches with the remnants of the traditional churches.

With all the churches around, is it necessary to prepare seminarians to teach people how to start groups, house churches, or whatever you want to call them? Yes, because one of the largest mission fields in the world is those in America and Europe who do not attend those churches. While the reasons for their absence differ greatly, there are a growing number who will not attend because the church is doing so little about the problems

12. Barna Group, "House Church Involvement Is Growing."

facing the world. Seminarians can get a good theological education and be introduced to politics of international justice, but where will they get the experience of the pain and suffering needed to give them a passion for their mission? Could it come from being a part of the many "churches of the dispersion," those churches that arise from Christian refugees continuing their culture and worship in a new land? There they will hear the stories of the refugees and migrants, their years in the camps, and their faith that got them through.

Should Pastor Kansa's son, Haro, make it to America, he will be part an Ethiopian church, perhaps worshipping in the Oromo language. People there know death and suffering. Not only have they experienced it, but they reverence the memory of Gudina Tumsa, a leader of their church who was martyred by their government for speaking out for the people against the government's atheistic rule.[13] This church of the dispersion knows both the simple joy of the gospel and its meaning for those in the agony of loss. For the American seminarian, the future apostolic missionary, experiencing the fellowship of refugees and maybe even a visit to their nation can foster a burning desire for ministry.

There is no one model for the Kingdom church. It might be a rural church willing to resettle refugees, a Communion service in a tent for those delivering wheat in Chad, a house church in Dallas demonstrating against an oil company, or a suburban congregation in Minneapolis building a water project in Guatemala. Much of this is happening now. As Jesus said, "The Kingdom of God is near."

---

13. Deressa and Wilson, eds. *The Life, Works, and Witness of Tsehay Tolessa and Gudina Tumsa,* xv-xxii.

Chapter 12

The Evangelism of Jesus

THEY MET IN THE basement of a church. It was a group of people who wanted to do something about climate change. Jane, the daughter of Pastor Mike, was there. The group had invited someone who had experienced the drought in East Africa. It was Pastor Kansa's son, Haro. He had made it through Europe to America. After the meeting they got to talking and Jane said, "Sometimes I get so discouraged. We don't seem to be making any progress." Haro said, "Yes, but my father always said, 'God will get us through all of this.' I'm here because all along my way there were people, so many, who helped with food, tents, and bandages. Without them we would never have made it." "But the drought, then the floods," she said, "When are we going fix that?" He replied, "As Jesus used people to get me here. He will use people like you to slow climate change."

The evangelism of Jesus was the good news that the Kingdom of God was at hand (Mark 1:15).[1] Pastor Kansa's son was translating that message, through his experience, that God's New World Society is at hand. God is using people to work toward fulfilling the promises of the Kingdom. Food for the world is grown, enriched, stored, transported, and provided for many of the world's neediest people. No, there is not enough, but people are working on that. Water is a worry. But there too, God uses engineers, hydrologists, agronomists, and statesmen seek to provide more pure water for all. God's New World Society is also made up of people in healthcare, and people providing low-cost housing, creating jobs, liberating the bound, and seeking peace.

---

1. Arias, *Announcing the Reign of God*, 2.

While the New World Society is near, it is only partial. Greed is pervasive, sin abounds, and evil often wins. Many die before their time in disasters and war. At its core God's New World Society embraces the death and resurrection of Christ, promising forgiveness for sinners and eternal life for the dying. This is why Paul directed his evangelism message directly about Christ when he said, "For I decided to know nothing among you except Jesus Christ, and him crucified" (1 Cor 2:2). Forgiveness and the resurrection is not only the message of pastors and priests; it is the everyday pardon going on in the household and the hope at a funeral. It also is the motive behind the Truth and Reconciliation Commission in South Africa and other countries. Christ's New World Society is holistic evangelization; it is good news for all areas of life.[2]

NO WAITING NECESSARY

One does not have to wait until an old regime is finished or a new president is elected. God's New World Society is consensual, not coercive. Christ is working through many people, bringing life and hope to people even though a government may be corrupt and uncaring. When asked when the Kingdom was coming, Jesus said, "The Kingdom of God is not coming with things that can be observed; nor will they say, 'Look, here it is!' or 'There it is!' For, in fact, the kingdom of God is among [or within] you" (Luke 17:20–21). You are invited to join, helping in any way you can, from serving food to protesting government policies. In every country and under any condition, you can do something to help. Christ is making you influential and you can mobilize soft power by attracting others to join you. Soft power works by drawing others to your goals by demonstrations of love, duty, and shared values.[3]

The New World Society even erodes polarization by appealing to universal values.[4] Nearly everyone applauds acts of love. When those acts of mercy impinge on someone else's selfishness, it is hard for them to complain too much. When some they are troubled by too many refugees entering their country, their God-given compassion confuses the matter. Yes, they are against wave after way of immigration, but their heart goes out to mothers and babies who have gone through so much. This is why

---

2. Arias, *Announcing the Reign of God*, 4.
3. Nye, *Soft Power*, 7.
4. Nye, *Soft Power*, 11.

worldwide immigration is causing so many problems. Not only has our reaction to immigration caused political divisions, but it has also caused a split within us as we weigh loyalty to our nation over against our concern for the suffering.

AMAZING WHEN WE SEE IT

We were amazed when the Berlin wall fell without a shot being fired. People cheered and leaped for joy. Was the world turning a corner? Maybe not, but at least good things are possible. When hungry Pakistan began exporting wheat, those who knew the global implications of this good news were now convinced that there was real hope for hungry people around the world. The nonviolent strategy of the civil rights movement, inspired by Kingdom goals, led to the Civil Rights Act. Liberation from oppression for African Americans was one step closer to realization.

All of this comes closer to home when a tornado strikes, fire destroys a whole town, floods wipe out a community. Then God's New World Society appears as neighbors who dig in to help and supply food, clothing, and shelter. Strangers arrive from afar to give a helping hand. Yes, climate caused the destruction, but the New World Society lent a helping hand for restoration. All of this reflects how "amazement" cuts through the numbness and says that good things are possible. Jesus' works of feeding, healing, and forgiving were not only incredible because they were miracles; they were amazing because they brought a new energy to the community.[5] Discouraged, John the Baptist asked about whether Jesus was even the Messiah. Jesus gave the amazing response, "Go and tell John what you have seen and heard: the blind receive their sight, the lame walk, the lepers are cleansed, the deaf hear, the dead are raised, m, the poor have good news brought to them" (Luke 7:22). The Kingdom was coming.

Amazement at what God is doing is also energizing when sinners repent and have their lives radically changed. An ex-drug dealer becomes a surgeon. A former prisoner counsels kids how to stay out of trouble. A high school dropout, at the end of his rope, is accepted by some of Jesus' friends. Then he goes back to school and now, with a PhD, teaches at the university. Examples like these are amazing and break open the possibility that change can also happen to us and others. Jesus reached down and saved them and

---

5. Brueggemann, *Prophetic Imagination*, 102.

turned them around. Quite likely, he did it through those people, who, for that purpose, were part of God's New World Society.

LIGHT IN THE DARKNESS

Nowhere does the New World Society seem as improbable as in devastation, destruction, oppression, and failing health. How could Jesus announce and demonstrate the promises of the Kingdom and then weep over the coming destruction of Jerusalem (Luke 19:41–44)? It was to be a repeat of the destruction of Jerusalem by Babylon, which Jeremiah prophesied. Since then, wars, famines, exploitation, slavery, and plagues have terrified and killed millions over the centuries. People ask, where is God's goodness, his grace, and the Kingdom? What is good about God's New World Society in tragedy?

For one thing, it makes us ask the question of whether we are at fault. Jeremiah laid the blame directly on the greed and lust of Judah's ruling class. Jesus said that Jerusalem had not known the time of God's visitation. Should capitalism come to an end or World War III break out, is it because the rich nations exploited the poor around the world? Is climate change the fault of those of us who have benefitted all these years from fossil fuel energy? For those who champion personal freedom over other concerns, is "freedom" another word for sheer selfishness? Any realization of the potential of the New World Society depends on repentance. Those in Christ will rejoice in forgiveness.

Another gift of God's New World Society is that Christ walks with us in the darkness. There is the terrible darkness of unexplained and unexplainable tragedy. Earthquakes devastate whole regions, burying innocent children. A tsunami kills thousands. A troubled youth opens fire and murders school children and their teacher. So much seems beyond our control. But it is in our helplessness that we can begin to find security—the security of a beggar. All that is left is the trust that he who died on the cross gives life to the dead and calls into existence the things that are not (Rom 4:17).[6] In that faith there flickers a weak candlelight. It is not enough to reveal much but gives just enough light for us to get to work.

---

6. Hall, *Lighten Our Darkness*, 119–20.

The Evangelism of Jesus

PROMISES KEEP US GOING

God is not going to fail us. Through the prophets, God promised forgiveness, food, water, and all the blessings of a new Kingdom. The people of Judah survived seventy years and started to come back. People in Russia and Eastern Europe waited and prayed for the atheistic government to end. Seventy years later it did. Oppression lets up; slaves are released and wars end. In this world the promises are never perfectly achieved but they keep us going. They also keep us going in the right direction.

For young people and those who have come to a crossroads in life, the promises of God provide a purpose in life. Fortunate are those who find a vocation that fits a promise directly. Nurses bring healing. Farmers provide food. Pastors forgive and bring the hope of the resurrection. Engineers help supply water and carpenters build houses. Politicians work for peace and an end to oppression. Not all are so fortunate to be so directly involved, yet Christ uses everyone in some way. The good news of the Kingdom of God is that you have a meaningful purpose in life. There is work to be done and Christ is calling you to join the party.

INTRODUCING THE KINGDOM

How might one tell others of the good news of the Kingdom, God's New World Society? With church membership declining, evangelism is seen as a very important task. In recent years a lot of attention has been given to how to introduce people to the good news. Some people who have a guilty conscience are introduced to Christ, who takes away sin. Others are asked, "If you were to die tonight, how do you think you can get into heaven?"[7] Campus Crusade asks people if they have heard the four spiritual laws. These approaches are good in pointing people to Christ as their Savior from sin and path to heaven. However, they feature only several aspects of the coming Kingdom. They also are somewhat individualistic and can sound like just proselytizing to the Christian faith.

Seeking to reach people with a more comprehensive view of Christ and the Christian faith, many have tried to make the church more attractive to others. Might it be the music? Should the church be more friendly? The idea is, "If they come, they will hear the gospel." Events are staged for the community and the evangelism committee has been replaced by a

---

7. Kennedy, *Evangelism Explosion*, 32.

marketing task force. However, people with wider concerns and worries on their minds may have other priorities than getting involved in a congregation and its committees.

Perhaps one of the best ways to introduce people to a conversation about the good news of the Kingdom came from an African American cab driver. When discussing the "how to" of evangelism, he said, "When those stressed folks get into my cab, I ask them, 'You got any hope'? Then I tell them why I have hope, and it isn't just about heaven; it is about what's going on all around us. I get to tell them about Jesus and why I also have hope for today."

Mortimer Arias speaks about why this hope is so important a message. He writes, "Here is where the annunciation of the Kingdom of hope becomes essential and important . . . Today, even the unbeliever can understand the limits and risks of history."[8] Given the sobering reality of our current crises, hope is crucial for both survival and action. But hope is not just an empty dream. Jürgen Moltman writes, "hopes and anticipations of the future are not a transfiguring glow imposed upon a darkened existence but are realistic ways of perceiving the scope of real possibilities, and as such, they set everything in motion."[9] To the inquirer, there is evidence that God is working through people to bring about the promises of the Kingdom. God's New World Society is accomplishing much. More needs to be done. Come join us.

AN UNLIMITED FUTURE

What about the unfinished tasks and the failure to help? Tragedies still happen and threats abound. Jesus said, "When you hear of wars and insurrections, do not be terrified; for these things must take place first, but the end will not follow immediately . . . Nation will rise against nation, and kingdom against kingdom; there will be great earthquakes, and in various places famines and plagues; and there will be dreadful portents and great signs from heaven" (Luke 21:9–11). Yet, these things are not the end. The disciples were not to be afraid; they would be saved. Others were to flee to find safety. Then when their death finally came, then they would see the Kingdom in all its final fulfillment. It had been there waiting for them since Christ's death and resurrection. It now waits for you. Jesus said, "And I saw

8. Arias, *Announcing the Kingdom*, 85.
9. Moltman, *Theology of Hope*, 25.

the holy city, the new Jerusalem, coming down out of heaven from God, prepared as a bride adorned for her husband. And I heard a loud voice from the throne saying, 'See, the home of God is among mortals. He will dwell with them; they will be his peoples, and God himself will be with them; he will wipe every tear from their eyes. Death will be no more; mourning and crying and pain will be no more, for the first things have passed away" (Rev 21:2–4).

AMAZED BY JOY

Telling others of the hope that is in you is more believable if you reflect the joy of the fellows Jesus described who discovered treasure in the field and the pearl of great price (Matt 13:44–46). The one digging in the field was truly surprised by what he found, like Christians who discover that their faith is not only a path to heaven but a way to confront their worries about the world around them. The man who discovered the pearl of great price is like one who has been searching for the meaning and purpose of life. Having found now the most important treasure of life is amazing and changes everything. It is worth giving up all your other valuables to have this joy. Reflecting that joy makes the hope that is in you believable.

Though the joy of the Kingdom provides the focus and zest for life, it is constantly tested. Jesus' disciples were thrilled that they had found the Messiah, but they still needed three years of instruction, observation, practice, and failure to learn what the Kingdom of God was all about. Making disciples is not just about church membership, as important as that might be. Making disciples means making replacements. As they had learned from hearing and watching Jesus, they were now called to do the same. As Jesus called them to be disciples, they were to call others. Yes, Bible classes are good, as are visiting the sick and homeless and volunteering in a poor nation. But evangelism is not complete without learning more about the Kingdom and doing Kingdom work. Sometimes learning more about the Kingdom means learning more from our fellow humans about how the world works. Just as Wallerstein's utopistics involves considering the limitations and constraints on possible utopias, Christians working with Christ on Kingdom goals will also need to consider worldly limitations and constraints. Working for the Kingdom is risky, like selling all you have to buy treasure in a field. But then you too can be amazed by joy.

The Last Kingdom Standing

WHERE DO WE START?

Christians differ as to what is most important in their mission and where to start. While all Christians wish to promote justice, alleviate hunger, attack ignorance and superstition, and help the victims of oppression, they disagree on the focus of their work. Evangelicals' chief concern is carrying the gospel across cultural boundaries to encourage those who have no allegiance to Christ to accept him as Lord and Savior and to become members of the church. Then, as the Holy Spirit leads, they work to evangelize others and work for justice in their society. They believe that the primary mission of the church is to evangelize the world and bring about the growth of the church. Evangelicals contrast their perspective with that of what they consider to be an ecumenical theology of mission.[10]

Ecumenical theology holds that the mission of God concerns everything that God is doing in the world. God is at work in all the religions of the world and the church can work alongside them as equals. The essence of evangelism is concerned with changing the structures of society that are evil. This means that it is more important to change social conditions than it is to convert individuals. Conversion is not about changing one's religious allegiance and system of belief. Instead, it is about turning away from self-seeking endeavors to those benefiting others. Social justice is the supreme task of the church, rather than to proclaim Christ as the only Savior of mankind. While ecumenical leaders protest that this is not a fair representation of their position, critics point to the fact that their allocation of resources shows this conclusion to be accurate.[11]

Defining the Kingdom as the realization of all of God's promises in the prophets, personal salvation and social welfare are two sides of the same coin. However, since both groups wish to work for the social welfare of the societies where they work, it raises the question of the place of feeding the hungry, healing the sick, and working for justice in a community and nation. If it is used as a lever to get people to believe in Christ, it raises some serious issues. This has long been condemned in some poor nations as "buying" Christians. Roland Allen put this into perspective when he wrote, "If the Good Samaritan had been an agent of the society established to propagate the doctrine that men should worship on Mount Gerizim, the

---

10. Braaten, *Apostolic Imperative*, 63–64.
11. Braaten, *Apostolic Imperative*, 64–66.

THE EVANGELISM OF JESUS

parable would have produced a different effect on those who heard it."[12] Jesus did not bargain with the people to believe in him so that they might be healed and fed. Nor should we.

Are we so absorbed in fixing society that we hope in the end that some people will catch on and then come to faith? That has not been successful in the Western world, nor on the mission fields in Asia, Africa, and Latin America. Allen pointed out that historically, while many people had been given an education in Christian schools and healed in Christian hospitals, the great mass of people were not drawn any nearer to Christ. He saw that the churches that supported social activities the most increased neither in numbers nor in spiritual power.[13]

CONVERSION

In Jesus' evangelism, "conversion" meant that people repented and believed all the good news of the Kingdom. The invitation came to both the religiously minded people and the outsiders. Today, it comes for Christians, people of other religions, and secularists. Repentance is for all sins but, in this case, especially those that have kept the promises of the Kingdom from being fulfilled. With respect to the inequality between rich and poor, the size of that division has been partially caused by Christians who "have a personal relationship with Jesus." For many Christians, "conversion" is a continuous process, like that experienced by Peter. Arias points out that Peter had a number of conversions. He left all and followed Christ (John 1:40–42). The second conversion was his realization that he was a sinful person in the presence of Jesus' power and authority (Luke 5:1–11). He came to a third conversion when he confessed that Christ was the Son of the living God (Mark 8:27–30). After his denial of Jesus, he was restored through his affirmation of love for Jesus (John 21:15–19). Then, even after his marvelous sermon at Pentecost, he still needed to be converted to see, in the matter of a Roman officer, that "Christ has no favorites" (Acts 10:34).[14]

In that light many of us Christians need to reevaluate our faith in reference to the Kingdom and see what other conversions God has in mind for us. Comfortable Christians might need to repent of partaking in the unjust division of wealth when through their commerce and politics they

---

12. Allen, "Place of Medical Missions," 34–42.
13. Allen, *Spontaneous Expansion of the Church*, 81.
14. Arias, *Announcing the Reign of God*, 114.

have profited from the exploitation of the poor. They may also need to be converted to believe the good news of the Kingdom that real progress can be made in correcting some of the social evils that they see all around them. It is not enough to say, "That is the way things are; that's life." In announcing the good news of the Kingdom, Jesus would say, "No, there is hope for the future."

For those of other faiths or no faith, especially those who are working diligently on social issues, conversion might be is seeing that real achievements of God's World Society are stymied without mutual forgiveness and the hope of life after death. Working together on disaster relief, feeding programs, water projects, and prison reform, Christians can share their faith and the source of their hope with their fellow workers. Ultimately Jesus is the "bread of life" (John 6:35). Again, he said, "Let anyone who is thirsty come to me" (John 7:37). As we worry about peoples' care and safety, we need to remember that Jesus announced, "I am the good shepherd. The good shepherd lays his life down for the sheep" (John 10:11). Finally, after the efforts to save lives fails, the Christian repeats what Jesus said: "I am the resurrection and the life. Those who believe in me, even though they die, will live, and whoever lives and believes in me will never die" (John 11:25).

As history unfolds and if we find ourselves in a transition to a different world system, we will be experiencing new levels of uncertainty and anxiety. Threats to our livelihood and security and even survival may define our future and that of our descendants. In this reality it will be difficult to see the Kingdom of God in its fullness. That is the way it was in Jesus' time. The words he said then are true today as well: "Very truly I tell you, no one can see the Kingdom of God without being born from above" (John 3:3). At another time he warned, "Truly I tell you, whoever does not receive the kingdom of God as a little child will never enter it" (Mark 10:15). Ah, but once you see the Kingdom in its fullness, for this life and the next, it is worth risking everything to buy the field and hold the pearl.

Conclusion

AFTER THEIR WARNING OF conflict and devastation, the prophets promised the blessings of the Kingdom of God. After Jesus foretold the destruction of Jerusalem, Jesus told his disciples more about the Kingdom. They shared that good news wherever they went. What if our present world system fades? While we may guess, we really do not know what will follow. The simple belief in progress, that the world is getting better, has all but disappeared. Because the future is a virtual blank slate, Wallerstein sees a need for "utopistics," creative ways of imagining the future. In a sense they are the mirror image of the promises of the prophets at the time of the destruction of Samaria and Judea. Like them, such utopistics cannot just be vague ideals unrelated to reality. Instead, they must be possible, even with limitations and constraints on achieving them. The aim is to analyze real alternatives to the present and seek to reconcile the searches for truth and for goodness.[1] The next twenty-five to fifty years may be terrible in terms of potential disasters and conflicts and a disintegration of our existing social system. Yet even this might lead to good news as people use faith and science for Kingdom goals. Then new solutions to old problems can emerge and new life from the ruins will arise.[2]

WORLD HISTORY

The promises of the Kingdom of God are a beautiful set of goals for utopistics in a new world system. They are rooted in a long world history. Their ideals and partial realization are found in the history of the Jews. Notable in this regard are the provisions for limiting the accumulation of wealth

---

1. Wallerstein, *End of the World*, 217.
2. Wallerstein, *End of the World*, 218–19.

through land reform, prohibitions on interest, and limits on slavery. While Jesus blessed the poor, he was harsh on the rich. Early Christians pursued these egalitarian goals through dramatic acts of sharing. Healing happened without money changing hands. In the terrors of conflicts, guilt and dying, Jesus' sacrifice and resurrection gained forgiveness and the hope for eternal life.

The Kingdom of God also played a prominent role in previous system shifts. When Rome fell, most of Europe lost its political and cultural center. Without the protection of Roman rule, security was scarce and education was limited. Writing *The City of God*, Augustine charted a way forward by incorporating elements of the Kingdom of God into his idea of a God-centered city. Soon thereafter, the pope served as a centralizing figure for the church and civilization of Europe. In chaotic circumstances, monasteries grew behind stout walls and, in Kingdom style, they integrated worship, learning, healthcare, agriculture, and hospitality to strangers.

In the transition between feudalism and capitalism protected by nation-states, Luther wrote of the Kingdom. In separating the Kingdom of God's grace from political kingdoms, he freed the nations' kings from the control of the church. Critics point out that he might have also freed them from moral constraints. In the system shift, many left the monasteries under the influence of the Reformation, while other monasteries were dissolved or taken over by the government. At the same time, Luther urged governments to promote education. This made school more available to the population under the state than it was under the church.

In the present world system, appeals to the goals of the Kingdom have helped millions. Some of the worst evils of colonialism were moderated. The slave trade was ended, and slaves were freed. More people are being fed because of progress in agriculture. Advances in medicine bring healing and extend the lives of people across the world. Forgiveness has helped to bring peace after war. Furthermore, the desire to end all war led to the creation of the League of Nations and then the United Nations. Motivated to save the lives of those impacted by climate change, people throughout the world are working to limit the rise in the temperature of the atmosphere. None of these efforts have been totally successful, yet they have made a significant difference in the lives of many. Confident in the promises of God and victory of Christ, Christians look forward to a perfect fulfillment of those promises in the life to come.

CONCLUSION

GOD'S NEW WORLD SOCIETY

Meanwhile, Christians join together and work with others in God's New World Society. Some states and political parties appeal to followers of a particular religion to gain power and cause divisions. At the same time leaders of those religions have joined with those of other faiths in detesting the divisions caused by their political leaders. As adherents of all religions respond to the needs of the poor and vulnerable around the world, they show by their deeds that they are united in some significant ways. God's New World Society is also made up of nongovernmental organizations, which have some of the most important roles in feeding the hungry and aiding thousands of refugees. Governments too, in their better moments, have brought water, energy, homes, jobs, and food to those who need it most. Urging them on for this work are also the advocates from religious and humanitarian groups who reflect Kingdom goals. Though united in their concerns, those making up the God's New World Society are not united in any other way. Is it time for an internet network linking together church charities, NGOs, UN commissions, and government agencies? While the evening news usually wants to close with a positive story, seldom do we hear of the resettlement of thousands, new water systems in arid communities, or breakthroughs in African agriculture. As news organizations close their international offices for lack of funds, a New World Society network providing news of positive developments would have real value.

This will become even more important as more nations turn to authoritarian, coercive governments to manage the coming crises. In the political face-off between Jesus and Pilate, it seemed as if Pilate had overwhelming power. Yet the soft power of love and concern for the weak was ultimately to prove more resilient and beneficial. This was the power of consensus, where people are impressed by fairness, freedom, and goodness. This soft power can be exerted even in totalitarian states. It was at the time of Jesus; it still is today in countries like China. It also draws together nations to work on common problems. Soft power is also manifest in nations coming together as they have in the European Union, the African Union, and others.

THE ENERGY TO CHANGE

Confronted by problems too big to fix, many are content to be distracted by the ordinary. That works fine until disaster comes too close to home.

Floods hit New York City. Gun shots ring out at the mall. Thousands cross the border. The ordinary begins to unravel and we get upset enough to do something. But what? Long before utopistics, the prophets painted pictures of everyone employed sitting under their own vine and fig tree; the deaf would hear and the lame would leap. The state could not do that, but God would. The pictures were unreal, yet had hope painted in the details. What might those pictures, those dreams, look like now? Some of the ills of capitalism would be healed if workers owned the corporations. Cashless medicine everywhere would do a better job of healing. Sun power in the desert would provide the energy to bring pure seawater for flowers and food. There will be cities of refuge instead of prison for many. Tables of food and fine wine will be there for those now hungry. Realistically the pictures are easy to dismiss, but our hopes are stirred; we wonder if there is a way to help. New energy emerges. Can we get to work? Will others join?

THE FUTURE BECKONS

The last vision is the best. All of the promises of the prophets have come to pass. It is all perfect; no weeds in the wheat; all the fish are good. We are welcomed by the King. His was the invitation and he brought us here. The valleys were lifted up and the hills were laid low. On his cross our failures were forgiven; in the empty tomb our hope was reborn. The Kingdom no longer is near. Now it is here.

With that vision of the future, we press on. Whether our church grows or folds, Christ's Kingdom is near. He has used cathedrals and house churches, monasteries and halfway houses. Leadership comes out of seminaries and also right out of the group. Money is not necessary, nor are buildings. Water is available for baptism, bread and wine for Communion. There is a special invitation for those at the edge of life, on the highways and byways. Sinners are welcomed and doubters are accepted.

My God, that is good news. It is worth sharing. In fact, it is hard to keep it to yourself. Pastor Mike, that was your message on Mark 1:15. Despite what is going on in your church, the nearness of the Kingdom is really good news. Pastor Kansa preached from the same text and said that the Kingdom *is* near, even in the drought and the war. Maybe there will be more food tomorrow, but there is always God's grace today, even if for some there will be no tomorrow.

Conclusion

THE END OF POLITICS AS USUAL

The Kingdom of God is the end of politics as usual. That was the meaning of Nebuchadnezzar's nightmare. He was the emperor of Babylon. He had stolen the treasures of the temple, killed a king, demolished Solomon's temple, killed thousands, and took Judah's elite into captivity. Like all emperors, he was concerned about his dynasty and its place in history. Now he had a terrible dream. There was a magnificent statue whose appearance was frightening. It had a head of gold, chest and arms of silver, a middle and thighs of bronze, and legs of iron. But the entire statue rested on feet of iron mixed with clay. Then a strange stone struck the feet and the immense statue crashed to the ground.

The prophet Daniel interpreted the dream as referring to the gigantic empires of the ancient world, beginning with Babylon (Dan 2:24–43). They governed enormous territories, equipped massive armies, enslaved thousands, and killed all who threatened their power. Daniel continued, "And in the days of those kings the God of heaven will set up a kingdom that shall never be destroyed, nor shall this kingdom be left to another people. It shall crush all these kingdoms and bring them to an end, and it shall stand forever" (Dan 2:44–45).

The Kingdom of God's soft power of consensus seems so weak in comparison with the coercive power exercised by authoritarian and, yes, even democratic politics. But it has already outlasted empires and dictatorships, wars and rumors of wars. It will triumph. Kingdom folk have fed and watered. They have healed and liberated; homes have been built and gardens planted. Some have been martyred. Some have been praised. Most have been ignored and forgotten. Yet they are a mighty movement, in every land and region. They remind us that the Kingdom is near. It will be *The Last Kingdom Standing*.

Bibliography

Albertus, Michael, and Victor Menaldo. *Authoritarianism and the Elite Origins of Democracy*. Cambridge: Cambridge University Press, 2018.
Allen, Roland. *The Ministry of Expansion: The Priesthood of the Laity*. Edited by J. D. Payne. Pasadena, CA: William Carey Library, 2017.
———. *Missionary Methods: St. Paul's or Ours?* London: World Dominion, 1956.
———. *The Spontaneous Expansion of the Church: And the Causes Which Hinder It*. Grand Rapids: Eerdmans, 1967.
Arias, Mortimer. *Announcing the Reign of God*. Philadelphia: Fortress, 1954.
Augustine. *The City of God: Against the Pagans*. Translated by Marcus Dobs. Peabody, MA: Hendrickson, 2020.
Bays, Daniel. *A New History of Christianity in China*. Chichester, UK: Wiley-Blackwell, 2012.
Barna Group. "House Church Involvement Is Growing." https://www.barna.com/research/house-church-involvement-is-growing/.
Barna, George, and David Kinnaman, eds. *Churchless: Understanding Today's Unchurched and How to Connect with Them*. Carol Stream, IL: Tyndale, 2014.
Berrigan, Daniel. *Isaiah: Spirit of Courage, Gift of Tears*. Minneapolis: Fortress, 1998.
Bharati, Dayanand. *Living Water in Hindu Bowl: An Analysis of Christian Failings in Communicating Christ to Hindus with Suggestions*. Pasadena, CA: William Carey Library, 2004.
Bhardwaj, Mayank. "India's Wheat Exports Hit a Record 7.85 Million Tons in 2021–2022 Trades." *Reuters*, April 4, 2022. https://www.reuters.com/world/india/indias-wheat-exports-hit-record-785-million-tonnes-2021-22-traders-2022-04-04/.
Bongmba, Elias, ed. *The Routledge Companion to Christianity in Africa*. New York: Routledge, 2018.
Bonhoeffer, Dietrich. *Ethics*. Translated by Reinhard Krauss. Minneapolis: Fortress, 2009.
Bornkamm, Heinrich. *Luther's Doctrine of the Two Kingdoms*. Philadelphia: Fortress, 1966.
Braaten, Carl. *The Flaming Center: A Theology of the Christian Mission*. Philadelphia: Fortress, 1977.
Branch, Taylor. *Parting the Waters: America in the King Years 1954–63*. New York: Simon and Schuster, 1988.
Bright, John. *The Kingdom of God: The Biblical Concept and Its Meaning for the Church*. Nashville: Abingdon, 1953.
Brueggemann, Walter. *The Land*. Philadelphia: Fortress, 1977.

Bibliography

———. *The Prophetic Imagination*. Minneapolis: Fortress, 2001.

Bultmann, Rudolph. "Introduction." In *Jesus' Proclamation of the Kingdom*, by Johannes Weiss. Mifflin Town, PA: Sigler, 1999.

Burge, Ryan. *The Nones: Where They Came From, Who They Are, and Where Are They Going*. Minneapolis: Fortress, 2021.

Buswell, Robert E., and Timothy S. Lee, eds. *Christianity in Korea*. Honolulu: University of Hawaii Press. 2016.

Carnegie Endowment for International Peace. "Water Way: How a Life-Sustaining Resource Goes Geopolitical." https://carnegieendowment.org/2022/03/22/water-war-how-life-sustaining-resource-goes-geopolitical-event-7843.

Center for the Study of Global Christianity. "Status of Global Christianity, 2023, in the Context of 1900–2050." Edinburgh: Gordon Cromwell Theological Seminary, 2023. https://www.gordonconwell.edu/wp-content/uploads/sites/13/2023/01/Status-of-Global-Christianity-2023.pdf.

Christian Network Europe. "The Secret Behind 1,000 New House Churches in Germany." May 26, 2023. https://cne.news/article/3118-the-secret-behind-1-000-new-house-churches-in-germany.

Collier, Stephanie. "War Anxiety: How to Cope." Harvard Health Publishihng, May 23, 2022. https://www.health.harvard.edu/blog/war-anxiety-how-to-cope-202205232748.

Cox, John Woodrow, et al. "More than 370,000 Students Have Experienced Gun Violence at School since Columbine." *Washington Post*, July 1, 2024 (updated). https://www.washingtonpost.com/education/interactive/school-shootings-database/.

Dalio, Ray. *The Changing World Order: Why Nations Succeed and Fall*. New York: Avid Readers, 2021.

Deressa, Samuel Yonas. " A Critical Approach to the Theology of the Ethiopian Evangelical Church, Mekane Yesus Known as Holistic Theology." *Journal of Gudina Tumsa Theological Forum* 1 (2015) 153–69.

Deressa, Samuel Yonas, and Sarah Hinlicky Wilson, eds. *The Life, Works, and Witness of Tsehay Tolessa and Gudina Tumsa, the Ethiopian Bonhoeffer*. Minneapolis: Fortress, 2017.

Dodd, C. H. *The Parables of the Kingdom*. New York: Scribner's, 1961.

Donovan, Vincent. *Christianity Rediscovered*. New York: Orbis, 1978.

Donkor, Audrey Elom. "Africa's Youth Unemployment Crisis Is a Global Problem." *Foreign Policy*, October 19, 2021. https://foreignpolicy.com/2021/10/19/africa-youth-unemployment-crisis-global-problem/.

Douglass, Frederick. *My Bondage and My Freedom*. New York: Penguin, 2003.

Dowsett, Rose. "Evangelicals and the Lausanne Movement." In *Evangelicals Around the World: A Global Handbook for the 21st Century*, edited by Brian Stiller, Todd M. Johnson, Karen Stiller, and Mark Hutchinson. Nashville: Thomas Nelson, 2015.

Emerson, P. J. *The Politics of Consensus: For the Resolution of Conflict and Reform of Majority Rule*. Belfast: Noel Murphy, 1995.

Engle, Richard, and Kennett Werner. "Steve Bannon and U.S Ultra-Conservatives Take Aim at Pope Francis." *NBC News*, April 12, 2019. https://www.nbcnews.com/news/world/steve-bannon-u-s-ultra-conservatives-take-aim-pope-francis-n991411.

Eskridge, Larry. "Evangelicals in North America." In *Evangelicals Around the World: A Global Handbook for the 21st Century*, edited by Brian Stiller, Todd M. Johnson, Karen Stiller, and Mark Hutchinson. Nashville: Thomas Nelson, 2015.

Bibliography

Fitzpatrick, Sean. "Leo the Great Versus Atilla the Hun." *Catholic Answers Magazine*, November 10, 2021, https://www.catholic.com/magazine/online-edition/leo-the-great-versus-attila-the-hun.

Forbes, F. A. *St. Vincent de Paul.* Gastonia, NC: TAN, 2021.

Franz, Erica. *Authoritarianism: What Everyone Needs to Know.* Oxford: Oxford University Press, 2018.

Gabbert, Adam. "Losing Their Religion: Why U.S. Churches Are on the Decline." *The Guardian*, January 22, 2023. https://www.theguardian.com/us-news/2023/jan/22/us-churches-closing-religion-covid-christianity.

Gaines, David. *The World Council of Churches.* Peterborough, NH: Noone, 1960.

Gottwald, Norman. *the Tribes of Yahweh: A Sociology of the Religion of Liberated Israel, 1250–1050 BCE.* Sheffield, UK: Sheffield Academic Press, 1999.

Grem, Darren. *The Blessings of Business: How Corporations Shaped Conservative Christianity.* New York: Oxford University Press, 2016.

Gutierrez, Gustavo. *Las Casas: In Search of the Poor of Jesus Christ.* Maryknoll, NY: Orbis, 1993.

———. *A Theology of Liberation: History, Politics, and Salvation.* Maryknoll, NY: Orbis, 1972.

Hall, John Douglas. *Lighten Our Darkness: Toward and Indigenous Theology of the Cross.* Philadelphia: Westminster, 1976.

Hengel, Martin. *Property and Riches in the Early Church: Aspects of a Social History of Early Christianity.* Philadelphia: Fortress, 1974.

Hesser, Leon. *The Man Who Fed the World.* Dallas: Durham, 2006.

Hickman et al., "Climate Anxiety in Children and Young People and Their Beliefs about Government Responses to Climate Change: A Global Survey." *The Lancet Planetary Health* 5:12 (December 2021). https://www.thelancet.com/journals/lanplh/article/PIIS2542-5196(21)00278-3/fulltext.

Hilkert, Mary Catherine, and Robert J. Schreiter. *The Praxis of the Reign of God: An Introduction to the theology of Edward Schillebeeckx.* New York: Fordham University Press, 2002.

Hollie, Marques. "Go Down Moshe: Decoding Negro Spirituals" *A Laboratory for Jewish Culture*, March 30, 2019. https://labajournal.com/2019/03/go-down-moshe/.

"House Church, the Fastest-Growing Expression of the Church." *Renewal Journal.* https://renewaljournal.com/2021/10/05/house-church-the-fastest-growing-expression-of-church/.

Huntington, Samuel. *The Clash of Civilizations: And the Remaking of World Order.* New York: Simon and Schuster, 1996.

Iberdrola. "Young People Rise Up against Climate Change." https://www.iberdrola.com/social-commitment/greta-thunberg-environmental-activist.

"Is the Cuban Health Care System Really as Great as People Claim?" *The Conversation*, November 30, 2016. https://theconversation.com/is-the-cuban-healthcare-system-really-as-great-as-people-claim-69526.

Isaacson, Walter. *Kissinger: A Biography.* New York: Simon and Schuster, 2005.

Inverleigh, Austen. *The Great Reformer: Francis and the Making of a Radical Pope.* New York: Holt, 2014.

Jeremias, Joachim. *Rediscovering the Parables.* Norwich, Norfolk, UK: Hymns Ancient and Modern, 2012.

Bibliography

Kaloudis, George. *Non-Governmental Organizations in the Global System.* London: Lexington, 2021.

Karlstrom, Nils. "Movements for International Friendship and Life and Work." In *A History of the Ecumenical Movement: 1517–1948,* edited by Ruth Rouse and Stephen Neill. Philadelphia: Westminster, 1967.

Kennedy, D. J. *Evangelism Explosion: Equipping Churches for Friendship, Evangelism, Discipleship, and Healthy Growth.* 4th ed. Carol Stream, IL: Tyndale, 1996.

Koesel, Karrie. *Religion and Authoritarianism: Cooperation, Conflict, and the Consequences.* New York: Cambridge University Press, 2014.

King, Martin Luther, Jr. *Where Do We Go from Here: Chaos or Community?* Boston: Beacon, 1968.

Kinnaman, David. *You Lost Me: Why Young Christians Are Leaving the Church and Rethinking Faith.* Grand Rapids: Baker, 2011.

Koester, Helmut. *History, Culture, and Religion of the Hellenistic Age: Introduction to the New Testament.* New York: De Gruyter, 1995.

Küng, Hans, and Karl-Josef Kuschel, eds. *A Global Ethic: The Declaration of the Parliament of the World's Religions.* New York: Continuum, 1993.

Lamb, Michael. *A Commonwealth of Hope: Augustine's Political Thought.* Princeton, NJ: Princeton University Press, 2022.

Landsberg, Chris. "Caught between Pan-African Solidarism and Realist Developmentalism: South Africa's Roll in the African Union." In *The African Union: Autocracy, Diplomacy, and Peacebuilding in Africa,* edited by Tony Karbo and Tim Murithi, 235–59, Cape Town: Tauris, 2020.

Latourette, Kenneth. *A History of Christianity.* New York: Harper, 1953.

———. *A Thousand Years of Uncertainty.* Vol. 2 of *A History of the Expansion of Christianity.* New York: Harper, 1953.

Macaskill, William. "The Beginning of History: Surviving the Era of Catastrophic Risk." *Foreign Affairs: The Centennial Issue* 101 (2022).

Masci, David. "Why Has Pentecostalism Grown So Rapidly in Latin America?" Pew Research Center, November 14, 2014. https://www.pewresearch.org/short-reads/2014/11/14/why-has-pentecostalism-grown-so-dramatically-in-latin-america/.

Mathews, Kuruvilla. "The African Union and the Renaissance of Pan-Africanism." In *The African Union, Autocracy, Diplomacy, and Peacebuilding in Africa,* edited by Tony Karbo and Tim Murithi. Cape Town: Tauris, 2018.

Mayfield, Danielle L. *Unruly Saint: Dorothy Day's Radical Vision and Its Challenge for Our Times.* Minneapolis: Broadleaf, 2022.

Meisler, Stanley. *United Nations: A History.* New York: Grove, 1995.

Mendenhall, George. *Ancient Israel's Faith and History.* Louisville: John Knox, 2001.

———. *The Tenth Generation: The Origins of the Biblical Tradition.* Baltimore: Johns Hopkins University Press, 1973.

Modelski, George. *Long Cycles in World Politics.* Seattle: University of Washington Press, 1987.

Moltmann, Jürgen. *Theology of Hope: On the Ground and the Implications of a Christian Eschatology.* Translated by James W. Leitch. Minneapolis: Fortress, 1993.

Noll, K. L. "Canaanitic Religion." *Religion Compass* 1:1 (2007) 61–92. https://people.brandonu.ca/nollk/canaanite-religion/.

Bibliography

Nye, Joseph. *Soft Power: The Means to Success in World Politics.* New York: Public Affairs, 2004.

Olique, David, ed. *Bertolome de las Casas, O.P.: History, Philosophy and Theology in the Age of European Expansion.* Leiden: Brill, 2019.

Olson, Jonathon. *The European Union: Politics and Promises.* New York: Routledge, 1921.

Perrin, Norman. *The Kingdom of God in the Teaching of Jesus.* Philadelphia: Westminster, 1963.

Pew Research Center. "Political Polarization in the American Public." June 12, 2014. https://www.pewresearch.org/politics/2014/06/12/political-polarization-in-the-american-public/.

Pomfret, John. *The Beautiful Country and the Middle Kingdom: America and China, 1776 to the Present.* New York: Holt, 2016.

Post, Kathryn. "Theological Schools Report Continued Drop in Master of Divinity Degrees." *Religious News Service*, December 2, 2022. http://www.religionnews.com/2022/12/02/theological-school-report-continues-drop-in-master-of-divinity-degrees/.

Pruitt-Young, Sharon. "Young People Are Worried about Climate Change." NPR, September 14, 2021. https://www.npr.org/2021/09/14/1037023551/climate-change-children-young-adults-anxious-worriedstudy.

Rauschenbusch, Walter. *The Righteousness of the Kingdom.* Edited by Max Stackhouse. Nashville: Abingdon, 1953.

Reinhart, Kurt. *Germany 2000 Years.* Vol. 1, *The Rise and Fall of the Holy Empire.* New York: Ungar, 1966.

Repucci, Sarah, and Amy Slipowitz. "The Global Expansion of Authoritarian Rule." Freedom House, 2022. https://freedomhouse.org/report/freedom-world/2022/global-expansion-authoritarian-rule.

Roach, David. "Church Attendance Dropped among Young People, Singles, Liberals." *Christianity Today*, January 2023. https://www.christianitytoday.com/news/2023/january/pandemic-church-attendance-drop-aei-survey youngpeople-eva.html.

Rosen, Corey, and Michael Querry. "How Well Is Employee Ownership Working?" *Harvard Business Review*, September 1987. https://hbr.org/1987/09/how-well-is-employee-ownership-working.

Rosling, Hans. *Factfulness: Ten Reasons Why We're Wrong about the World and Why Things Are Better than You Think.* New York: Flat Iron, 2018.

Rukato, Hesphina. "The African Union: Regional and Global Challenges." In *The African Union, Autocracy, Diplomacy, and Peacebuilding in Africa*, edited by Tony Karbo and Tim Murithi, 109–17. Cape Town: Tauris, 2020.

Schlatter, Adolf. *The Church in the New Testament Period.* London: SPCK, 1961.

Schmidt, Robert. "The Legitimacy of Revolution: The World Council of Churches' Grants to the Liberation Movements in Southern Africa." PhD diss., University of Washington, 1983.

———. "The Ministry of Expansion and Contemporary Crises." In Roland Allen, *The Ministry of Expansion: The Priesthood of the Laity*, edited by J. D. Payne. Pasadena, CA: William Carey Library, 2017.

———. *Water Management in West Pakistan.* Peshawar: Pakistan Academy for Rural Development, 1971.

Schweitzer, Albert. *The Quest for the Historical Jesus.* Vancouver, BC: Kshetra, 2016.

Schwiebert, E. G. *Luther and His Times.* St. Louis: Concordia, 1951.

BIBLIOGRAPHY

Shattuck, John, and Kathryn Sikkink. "Practice What You Preach, Global Human Rights Leadership Begins at Home." *Foreign Affairs* 100 (2021) 150–60.

Sider, Ron. "Evangelicals and Social Justice." In *Evangelicals Around the World: A Global Handbook for the 21st Century*, edited by Brian Stiller, Todd M. Johnson, Karen Stiller, and Mark Hutchinson. Nashville: Thomas Nelson, 2015.

Simson, Wolfgang. "House Church Global Report." *Simple Church Journal*, July 2021. https://www.simplechurchjournal.com/2021/07/house-church-global-report-by-simson.html.

Starr, Chester. *History of the Ancient World*. New York: Oxford University Press, 1977.

Stiller, Brian. "An Introduction to the World Evangelical Alliance." In *Evangelicals Around the World: A Global Handbook for the 21st Century*, edited by Brian Stiller, Todd M. Johnson, Karen Stiller, and Mark Hutchinson. Nashville: Thomas Nelson, 2015.

Strauss, Leo, and Joseph Cropsey. *History of Political Philosophy*. Chicago: Rand McNally, 1972.

Tompkins, Stephen. *William Wilberforce: A Biography*. Grand Rapids: Eerdmans, 2007.

Tromp, Johannes. *The Assumption of Moses: A Critical Edition with Commentary*. New York: Brill, 1993.

UNHCR. "Basic Needs Approach to the Refugee Response." May 2018. https://www.unhcr.org/blogs/wp-content/uploads/sites/48/2018/05/Basic-Needs-Approach-in-the-Refugee-Response.pdf.

———. "Refugee Statistics." https://www.unrefugees.org/refugee-facts/statistics/.

United Nations. "Food." https://www.un.org/en/global-issues/food.

United Nations News. "In Afghanistan Women Take Their Lives Out of Desperation." July 2022. https://news.un.org/en/story/2022/07/1121852.

United States Chamber of Commerce. "What Is an Employee Owned Company?" https://www.uschamber.com/co/run/finance/what-is-an-employee-owned-company.

Wallerstein, Immanuel. *The End of the World as We Know It: Social Science for the Twenty-First Century*. Minneapolis: University of Minnesota Press, 1999.

———. *World Systems Analysis: An Introduction*. Durham, NC: Duke University Press, 2006.

Watson, Bryan. *Headed into the Abyss: The Story of Our Time and the Future We'll Face*. Swampscott, MA: Anvilside, 2019.

Weiss, Johannes. *Jesus' Proclamation of the Kingdom*. Mifflin Town, PA: Sigler, 1999.

Welsh, David. *The Rise and Fall of Apartheid*. Charlottesville: University of Virginia Press, 2009.

White, James. *The Rise of the Nones: Understanding and Reaching the Religiously Unaffiliated*. Grand Rapids: Baker, 2014.

World Evangelical Alliance. www.worldea.org/what-we-do/global-advocacy.

World Vision. www.org/our-partners/world-evangelical-alliance.

Wright, N. T. *How God Became King: The Forgotten Story of the Gospels*. New York: HarperOne, 2011.

———. *Simply Jesus: A New Vision of Who He Was and Why It Matters*. New York: HarperOne, 2011.

Wright, William. *Martin Luther's Understanding of the Two Kingdoms*. Grand Rapids: Baker, 2010.

Yeats, William. "The Second Coming." In *Modern Verse*, edited by Oscar Williams. New York: Washington Square, 1974.

www.ingramcontent.com/pod-product-compliance
Lightning Source LLC
Chambersburg PA
CBHW051108160426
43193CB00010B/1367